blind
spots

Why Students Fail...
and the Science That Can Save Them

Kimberly Nix Berens, Ph.D.

THE
collective.
BOOK STUDIO

ISBN: 978-1-951412-09-8
Ebook ISBN: 978-1-951412-10-4
LCCN: 2020906709

Manufactured in the United States of America.

Design by Happenstance Type-O-Rama.

10 9 8 7 6 5 4 3 2 1

The Collective Book Studio
Oakland, California
www.thecollectivebook.studio

For Maria,
who taught me to
see my blind spots.

CONTENTS

INTRODUCTION

It was a scene with which I am all too familiar: a mother in tears after a school meeting about her child's academic struggles. The meeting was filled with professionals of all types: her child's classroom teacher, the special education teacher, the head of special education services for the district, the school psychologist, the school principal . . . and me, a behavioral educator who had been providing her child with private reading intervention services every day after school for 40 hours over eight weeks.

One year before this meeting, her child, whom I will call Alex, had been classified as dyslexic by the district's school psychologist, which qualified him for special education services. Alex was in first grade at the time of his diagnosis. He began receiving specialized reading instruction during each school day, where he was pulled out of his regular class to work with a special education teacher. After more than six months of this intervention, mom had seen no improvement in his reading skills. Moreover, Alex had begun to completely withdraw socially and had become increasingly anxious about completing his schoolwork or going to school altogether. It was around this time that the school psychologist and special education teacher informed her that, as a means of reducing his frustration and anxiety, she needed to accept that Alex might never learn to read well due to his disability and that she should give him access to audio recordings of books rather than having him attempt to read.

Fortunately, mom decided to take matters into her own hands at that point, and as luck would have it, she discovered my organization and enrolled her son for private after-school reading intervention. I initially conducted a core reading skills assessment with Alex, an assessment I developed that precisely identifies a child's mastery of essential skills for reading, like identifying the sounds of letters, discriminating between vowels and consonants, and sounding out words. From this assessment, it was clear to me that Alex had never mastered the essential skills for reading. He was unable to identify letter sounds or use phonics to decode unknown words. Moreover, he had gotten really good at some really bad habits—bad habits that his teachers had specifically trained him to do, like looking at the first letter of a word and guessing the word based on a picture or context clues. Thus, Alex was an extraordinarily good *word guesser*. He had learned and become masterful at exactly what his teachers had taught him to do—guess words. He then received a diagnosis of dyslexia because, naturally, he often guessed words incorrectly, even though he was doing exactly as he had been taught.

After 40 hours with me, Alex had made significant gains in his fluency in phonics, his ability to use phonics to decode unknown words, and his overall reading fluency. He had begun reading with mom at home and had started reading things in his natural environment like road signs, menus at restaurants, and billboards. He had also become more confident and was engaging in the world again—laughing, smiling, coming out of his shell. He was finally experiencing success as a reader. Mom was thrilled with his progress. However, I was still trying to unwind his word-guessing history. Getting rid of old habits and replacing them with effective reading skills requires lots and lots of practice. Thus, we needed to increase his hours to ensure that we could accelerate his skills rapidly enough that he could begin the next school year on grade level. Moreover, we needed to make sure that he wasn't being provided with reading intervention that reinforced his word-guessing habits.

In order to manage an increase in hours with me, mom asked for the meeting to request that he be allowed to discontinue the special education services with the school and attend sessions with me instead, as a modified school day. Since I'm an educator trained as a behavioral scientist, I arrived at the meeting with a wealth of data showing his progress, as well as data that clearly indicated how his old word-guessing habits were interfering with his mastering effective reading strategies. We presented our case to the team and held our breath. The rest of the meeting was no different than all the other school meetings of this sort I have attended throughout my career. The data were irrelevant. My expertise was irrelevant. His progress wasn't real. Mom's heartfelt pleas fell on deaf ears.

From the team's perspective, Alex was a dyslexic and would always be a dyslexic. Any progress he was making with me would never show up in the classroom. My methods were confusing him because they weren't the same as those used by his teachers. I was the problem. My methods were the problem—even though the data clearly indicated otherwise. The members of that team *believed* that Alex was disabled, and they also *believed* in the way they were teaching him. The meeting became an ideological debate, with the evidence regarding the effectiveness of my work with him and the progress he had made ignored and, worse, erroneously refuted.

So, there mom and I were in the parking lot after an excruciatingly frustrating meeting. They had denied her request to discontinue the ineffective reading intervention he was receiving at school as well as her request for a modified school day to attend more sessions with me. Mom was beside herself. As we walked to our cars, she stopped me and with hopeless fury asked, "Why don't they understand this? Why can't they see that what you're doing is working? Why don't more people know about your methods, your science? How can this continue to be ignored?" I hugged her, sharing in her pain and frustration. I had experienced scenes like this one countless times in my career, but it never got any easier. I assured her that we would continue to make progress, that there was absolutely nothing *wrong* with Alex, that he just needed to master basic skills with repeated, reinforced practice. I told her, "Alex will be a proficient, confident reader—you have my word on that." Before we got into our cars, she turned to me and said, "You know what you need to do? You need to write a book. The world needs to know about this."

I wrote this book because, like Alex's mom, I am angry. I am fed up. I am exhausted by the incessant spinning of wheels. I am heartbroken by the countless children I encounter who have been tragically failed or mediocritized by our educational system—a system that fails to effectively educate more than 60% of American students by the time they graduate.[1] I am devastated after my conversations with parents who feel overwhelmed and confused about how to help their children simply survive school. I am outraged for every American teacher who is charged with the task of effectively educating our nation's youth without ever being provided with training in the scientific tools required to do so. I am sick and tired of hearing about yet another educational fad or reform effort that has absolutely no chance of improving educational practices.

However, an answer to our educational crisis does exist. I am one of a group of scientist-educators who actually have an answer, and we have had an answer for a very long time. A science exists that allows children to learn as individuals even though they must be educated in groups. A science exists that avoids senseless labels that sentence children to lifetimes of failure and mediocrity.

Since 1998, I have been developing an organization called Fit Learning, where we use behavioral science and its corresponding Technology of Teaching[2, 3] to rapidly accelerate the core academic and cognitive skills of learners. I co-founded this organization as a doctoral student in behavioral science. During my undergraduate training at Rollins College, I won the metaphorical lottery when I met my mentor, a brilliant behavioral scientist who set me on my path in this field. Through her I quickly got a job in a residential treatment facility where I was trained to apply behavioral principles to improve the quality of life for profoundly disabled adults. From there, I was recruited by another mentor to help start a preschool for children with autism. My early work in the field involved applications of our science to disabled populations, and the results of that work were astounding. I was hooked. I chose to pursue doctoral training and was accepted into the Behavior Analysis Program at the University of Nevada, Reno (UNR).

In graduate school I initially continued my work in autism and served as director of the UNR Early Childhood Autism Program. Although I was continually amazed by the impact our science could make on the lives of children with autism and other disabilities, I became increasingly shocked at its narrow impact. Of course, the lives of children with disabilities matter and behavioral methods greatly improve their quality of life, but our science was nowhere to be found in mainstream education.

So in 1998 I got together with two other like-minded graduate students, and we started an after-school math program. The only space we could get on campus was an empty janitor's closet that we converted into a makeshift session room, and the only students we initially worked with were children of UNR faculty. Of course, we used applied science to develop and improve our methods, so as news of the amazing outcomes we were producing started to spread, other parents in the community enrolled their kids. We developed a reading program in addition to math and, as we grew, the university gradually gave us bigger classrooms, and eventually, a lecture hall in which to run sessions. More graduate students became involved and before we knew it, we had established a successful university-based tutoring program employing instructional methods guided by behavioral science and the Technology of Teaching. We were even the subject of an article in the *Reno Gazette Journal.*

As word of mouth about the effectiveness of our program spread, parents began taking their children out of the literacy program run by the Department of Education at UNR and enrolling them in ours instead. This did not please prominent members of the education department, and in 2002 we were told to shut down our program. From their perspective, behavioral scientists had no business working with kids in academic areas. The Department of Education held a lot of power in the university, a lot more than the Behavior Analysis Program. The faculty in the Department of Education were influential members of the establishment. The faculty in the Behavior Analysis Program were not. Although we were producing measurably superior outcomes compared with the education-based literacy program, our outcomes didn't matter. We were stepping on some very powerful toes and needed to go away.

I was devastated. I had built that program from the very beginning—volunteering my time and using my own money to buy materials. My husband, Nick, had gotten involved early on as well, so we decided to approach the university about privatizing the program off campus. The behavior analysis faculty had supported this project from its inception and agreed that it needed to survive and thrive. So with their approval, Nick and I took a big risk and started a company while completing our doctoral degrees (and also raising a daughter who had come into our lives by this time). Many people thought we were nuts!

However, from our humble beginnings running sessions out of a converted janitor's closet, we now offer a formal, competency-based certification in our method. Fit Learning has grown to over 30 locations worldwide with hundreds of learners enrolled each year. Our learners consistently achieve more than one year of growth after only 40 hours of instruction, and we produce these gains with every type of student, even the most challenged.

Throughout my career, I have spoken with hundreds of parents like Alex's mom, who come to me with a very similar story: Their children are struggling in their current school settings because they are not effectively learning to read, write, think, or do math. A large number of these kids have been classified, or are on their way to being classified, as having a learning disability. In other words, because these kids are failing to learn in their current educational environments, it is presumed that there is something inherently wrong with them.

Throughout the evolution of Fit Learning, the circumstances of our educational system have not changed. Educational reform has been a persistent theme in American education since the beginning of the 20th century.[4, 6] Decade after decade, various reforms have been tried and all have failed. I know that such persistent failure seems impossible to comprehend. Yet in over a century of educational reform, not a single effort has resulted in the majority of school children being educated effectively. I wrote this book with the hope that it will reveal the real reasons our educational system fails, which are very different from what people generally believe.

One of the most meaningful aspects of my job is when I get to create a distinction for a parent. A distinction occurs when we learn something we never knew before. When we realize something that *we did not know we did not know*. In other words, we discover something that I like to call *blind spots*. Imagine going through your entire life thinking that vanilla is the most delicious flavor of ice cream, because you didn't know chocolate existed. Suddenly someone hands you a chocolate ice cream cone. What a mind-blowing experience, right? Those are the kinds of moments I try to create for parents. I try to help parents see their blind spots. I try to create distinctions about possibilities for their children that they haven't had the opportunity to consider before. A lot of power comes from moments like these. Power to make a change. Power to make things better. Power to make a difference.

I wrote this book to help you discover your blind spots. To create distinctions for you about the many reasons students fail—the causes for failure that the establishments never tell you because they don't necessarily have these distinctions either. Members of the establishments have blind spots too. Academic failure, more often than not, has absolutely nothing to do with what most believe to be its cause—that something is wrong with the student.

Behavioral science has led us to discover the many variables that impact whether or not learning occurs. Though not recognized by the establishments, behavioral science is the science of learning. As I will explain in detail, we have evolved to learn through a very specific process: the repeated reinforcement of our behavior over time. As our behavior occurs and comes into contact with reinforcing consequences in our environment, it increases in rate—becomes faster—until it is established as a permanent part of our repertoire. In other words, with enough repeated reinforcement over time, behavior becomes habitual. There are many factors that enhance and interfere with this process, but virtually none of them have anything to do with disabilities or dysfunctions inherent in learners. Learners fail to learn because of ineffective learning environments.

In this book, I am going to create distinctions for you around how we got into this mess in the first place. As I mentioned previously, more than 60% of American students graduate below proficiency, which increases to over 80% for students of color and those living in poverty.[1] With statistics like these, I'm pretty confident in declaring that American education is an absolute mess.

In the first chapter, I will attempt to illustrate the significance of this problem. I assure you, our educational crisis is extremely grave. It poses not only a substantial threat to the future of our nation but threatens the very survival of the human race. In Chapter 2, I will introduce you to the establishments—the beliefs, traditions, and practices that shape education in this country. I will lead you through the complex history of our educational system to illustrate how ingrained cultural beliefs have led to education's systemic ineffectiveness. In Chapter 3, I will introduce you to behavioral science and illustrate the power it holds to transform the effectiveness of educational practices. I will also share the frustration of its continued suppression by the many establishments that are, and have always been, in charge. In Chapters 4 and 5, I will describe the traditions that dominate our nation's schools, as well as expose the myths that have been invented to account for the fact that these educational traditions fundamentally don't work. In Chapter 6, I will introduce you to the Technology of Teaching and contrast this approach with the ineffective instructional practices that dominate our nation's schools. Finally, in Chapter 7, I will offer compelling evidence about the superior outcomes that instructional methods guided by behavioral science and the Technology of Teaching have historically produced, although this evidence has been repeatedly ignored or erroneously refuted by the establishments.

I offer you this information primarily because I want you to know that it exists. I do not expect you to become behavioral scientists after reading this book and acquire the skills to provide this kind of instruction to your own children, or to your students if you happen to be teachers. As I have said, our field has been consistently silenced and ostracized by the mainstream establishments. The termination of our highly effective academic program at UNR clearly illustrates that point. I offer you this information to empower you to be better advocates for your children and students—to provide you with the means to pause and consider other possibilities when children in your lives struggle or fail, rather than immediately assuming something must be wrong with them. I offer you this so that more learners have a chance—a chance to acquire the kind of skills and expertise that will allow them to be confident, joyful, vital, successful and, eventually, capable of making a profound difference in the world. We have a lot of problems to solve and we need a lot of well-educated people to solve them.

The beliefs, traditions, and practices of the many establishments that influence education in this country are intractable. Therefore, the pressure to evolve is going to have to come from the outside—from citizens who share our belief that every child has the right to an effective education,[7] one that is as scientifically sound and technically precise as the medical care we expect from a doctor. I maintain that such a Technology of Teaching exists, yet the establishments consistently block its implementation in our nation's schools. It's time to call this situation what it is: a national scandal of epic proportions, a shameful failure of our democracy. And in education, as on so many other fronts in our society right now, we are quickly running out of time.

A Note to the Reader

I want to alert readers to the unique referencing system used throughout the book. The superscripted numbers that appear like footnotes actually refer to citations rather than notes. The reference list is numbered according to when that citation is first referenced in the book, and these superscripted numbers that appear throughout the book match the numbered references that appear at the end of the book. You can find the referenced citation by matching the superscripted number to the numbered reference list at the end of the book. I chose to use numbers rather than the authors' names in the reference because the book is highly referenced, and I felt that long lists of authors' names might disrupt the flow for the reader. The numbering system allowed me to comprehensively reference the book without distracting from its content.

You may also come across some unfamiliar terms throughout the book. I tend to use "learner" a lot, which as defined means "one who learns." I prefer the term "learner" to the term "student," because "learner" implies an active learning process rather than a passive experience that simply happens to a person, which "student" tends to imply. My hope is that as you read the book, you will gain an understanding as to why such a distinction is important.

I also use the term "establishments" throughout the book. Many of you may be familiar with the singular "establishment" but may be unclear as to why I use this term in its plural form. As I attempt to clarify throughout the book, I use "establishments" to refer to the beliefs, practices, traditions, and myths that dominate our culture — of which there are many. As such, I feel that the plural form "establishments" best characterizes the phenomena that have so greatly influenced our educational system.

I also introduce some terms that stem from behavioral science with which most of you will be unfamiliar. I have done my best to define these terms in the book when I introduce them. I know coming across unfamiliar terminology can be a bit scary, but I felt it important to use these terms to most clearly articulate our powerful science for all of you.

1

THE CRISIS

"The most widely publicized efforts to improve education show an extraordinary neglect of method. Learning and teaching are not analyzed, and almost no effort is made to improve teaching. . . ."
—B. F. SKINNER[2]

In October 2019, I attended a press conference about the results of the most recent National Assessment of Educational Progress (NAEP), which evaluated the reading and math achievement of 4th and 8th graders. Prior to this event, I had spent a good deal of time analyzing data from previous cycles of this test, which is typically administered every two years with 4th and 8th graders and every four years with 12th graders. I am quite familiar with the abysmal results of previous testing cycles, so I didn't have high hopes for the 2019 results.

During the press event, the associate commissioner of the NAEP presented highlights from the 2019 test. The good news: Fourth graders gained one point in math as compared with the 2017 test. The bad news: Scores decreased by one point for 8th graders in math, and scores decreased by multiple points for both 4th and 8th graders in reading. Moreover, lower-performing students, or those scoring in the 25th percentile or below, showed further declines in performance, while higher-performing students, or those scoring above the 50th percentile, stayed the same or showed some improvement. In other words, the achievement gap between high and low performers has gotten wider, and struggling students are performing even worse than they had in previous years.

I found several aspects of the press conference troubling. First, results were presented in such a way that it was not easy to interpret what they actually meant. No reference was made to what percentage of students scored as below proficiency, proficient, or advanced. The 2019 scores were presented in comparison only with the 2017 scores. Without knowing how scores relate to proficiency levels, the data may not seem that alarming. Math scores for 8th graders decreased by only one point and reading scores for both 4th and 8th graders only decreased by a few points. No big deal, right?

Actually, these declines really are a big deal. They are a big deal because these scores reflect performance well below the proficient level.[1] In other words, on average, 4th and 8th graders scored well below proficiency in math and reading. That one-point gain in 4th grade math scores still did not lead to average scores at the proficient level. And those decreases in 4th and 8th grade reading scores reflect performances that have dropped even further below proficiency. Unfortunately, results weren't described in this way. Without understanding that average scores are still well below proficiency, the public is probably left far less alarmed than they should be.

The associate commissioner offered only one possible explanation for the decline in test scores: a serious shortage of school supplies.

Apparently, exit surveys of teachers whose students participated in the 2019 NAEP cited a lack of school supplies as the most significant factor affecting their ability to teach effectively. Seems like a pretty oversimplified explanation for such abysmal test scores, which might lead to the natural conclusion that if we just had enough pencils, paper, and other materials in the classroom, everything would be fine! I'm not sure what bothered me more — that the associate commissioner of the NAEP didn't have more to offer in terms of analyzing the inadequacies of our educational system, or that so many American teachers think a lack of school supplies is the reason for systemic academic failure.

Finally, toward the end of the press conference, the associate commissioner said, "It appears that we just don't know how to move scores for reading." She made this statement in response to a question posed by a member of the press about consistently declining reading scores. As someone who has been dramatically accelerating reading achievement for more than 20 years, I find statements of this sort to be absolutely infuriating. It's clear that the educational establishment does not know how to move reading achievement scores. However, educators informed and guided by behavioral science and the Technology of Teaching have been dramatically increasing reading achievement for decades.[8, 9] As we'll see, Fit Learning produces average gains in reading of more than 30 percentile ranks in 40 hours of instruction. This statistic reflects greater gains than most American students make in an entire school year. *We* actually do know how to move reading scores.

I left that press conference disheartened. Our nation's schools consistently fail to effectively educate our nation's youth. Changing teaching practices and the educational system as a whole poses an enormous challenge, even to the most determined and well-intentioned. To get people to move mountains, they first need to be convinced that those mountains require moving.

As I stated earlier, American education is an absolute mess. I know that may sound inflammatory or overly critical, but a powerful declaration must be made in order to raise the necessary alarm. Sugar-coating abysmal test scores and sweeping the problem under the rug are recurring practices by the establishments, misleading the public into believing progress has been made when it hasn't been, or drawing attention away from how horrifying the problem actually is. So, a word of warning — I won't be sugarcoating anything. Revolutions don't come from apathy. Revolutions stem from outrage.

I will demonstrate that the state of education in our country reflects an ongoing crisis that impacts every student regardless of age, socio-economic level, race, ethnicity, gender, classification, or type of school. The educational crisis has implications for the future of our nation as devastating as natural disasters, economic meltdowns, and disease outbreaks. Unfortunately, the educational crisis doesn't receive a fraction of the economic resources or nationwide attention as other such calamities.

Our country has apparently grown accustomed to the inability of a majority of American students to compete on national or international tests of academic competency, because this lack of proficiency has been a recurring theme throughout the history of our school system. Despite frequent reference to the "good old days" of schooling, typically identified as that period following World War II, such recollections are not supported by historic achievement data.[4] I will demonstrate that there has never been a time in our nation's history when a majority of schoolchildren scored at or above proficient levels in academic subjects — or that a significant percentage were able to score at advanced levels. This romantic vision of effective schooling in the past has no basis in reality. School doesn't work for a majority of students, and it never has. What follows is a collection of alarming statistics regarding the tragic failure of American schools. For those interested in a more in-depth analysis of current educational trends, detailed figures reflecting the statistics I describe below are available on my website at www.drkimberlyberens.com.

NATIONAL ASSESSMENT OF EDUCATIONAL PROGRESS (NAEP)

Students Become Less Proficient the Longer They Spend in Our School System

In America, proficiency rates actually decline over the course of schooling. Yes, you read that sentence correctly. The more schooling an American student gets the less proficient they become. With the exception of reading, performance across all academic domains generally declines across the grade levels. In other words, a smaller percentage of 12th graders score as proficient than 8th graders, and a smaller percentage of 8th graders score as proficient than 4th graders. For example, on the most recent NAEP for mathematics, 41% of 4th graders scored as proficient but only 34% of 8th graders and 25% of 12th graders scored as proficient.[1] These declining trends across the grade levels also hold true for science, civics, U.S. history, and geography. Slightly more 12th graders do score as proficient in reading than 4th and 8th graders; however, despite this slight improvement over time, less than 40% of 12th graders graduate as proficient in reading.

These statistics are beyond shocking. One could reasonably assume that mastery of more advanced skills and content in the later grades builds upon the skills acquired in previous grades. If schooling is effective, students should become more proficient over time, not less. However, the longer students spend in our school system, the less proficient they become in essential academic areas.

Conversely, teaching practices guided by behavioral science and the Technology of Teaching produce *true mastery* of basic academic skills, which then leads to the effective learning and mastery of more complex skills.[10-13] As you read this book, it will become clear that permanent learning occurs through the repeated, reinforced practice of skills over time, and more advanced skills can only be effectively learned when prerequisite skills have been truly mastered.

Unfortunately, our schools aren't designed this way. Rather, students are pushed along through the grade levels based on age and the passage of time without regard to whether or not mastery of prerequisite skills has been achieved. The tragic result of this practice is evidenced by the statistics I just presented. They indicate that without true mastery of essential skills in the primary grades, American students cannot effectively learn and master skills required in middle and high school.

Our Educational System Tragically Fails Children of Color and Those Living in Poverty

Our school system fails black, Hispanic, and Native American students more significantly than white or Asian students. Of all racial and ethnic groups, schools fail black students the most consistently with more than 90% graduating below proficiency in math and science and more than 80% graduating below proficiency in reading. Hispanic and Native American students aren't faring much better. More than 80% graduate below proficiency in math and science and more than 70% graduate below proficiency in reading. In comparison, close to 70% of white students graduate below proficiency in math and science, and 54% graduate below proficiency in reading. Asian students tend to outperform all groups, with 52% graduating below proficiency in math, 62% graduating below proficiency in science, and 51% graduating below proficiency in reading. Although a majority of students in all racial and ethnic groups are below proficiency in all subjects, this percentage is much greater for students of color.

These findings reflect the historic inequity in educational opportunity for children of color in America. Eighty years after the civil rights movement, children of color continue to be overwhelmingly failed by our nation's schools. Although federal law prohibits segregation, our schools largely remain segregated due to entrenched racism in America.[14, 15] White people tend to move away from, or avoid moving into, minority communities, leaving those neighborhood schools attended mainly by children of color. Moreover, gentrification of urban areas and redistricting or rezoning practices tend to promote segregation.

Communities impacted by these practices also tend to be economically disadvantaged.[14, 15] The interconnectedness of race and class in America has devastating effects on neighborhood schools, which are primarily funded by local property taxes. The more impoverished the neighborhood, the less money available for schools. So not only are minority children victims of ineffective teaching practices, they also cannot even access clean, safe school facilities with proper plumbing, heating and cooling systems, updated textbooks in good repair, computer technology, or standard school supplies. Minority children have the deck stacked against them in every way, and this fact is devastatingly apparent in their NAEP scores.

When NAEP scores are evaluated with respect to socioeconomic level rather than race, similar inequities are apparent. More than 80% of low-income 8th graders scored below proficiency in reading and math in 2019. These data equate to less than 20% of low-income students achieving the proficient level and less than 5% achieving the advanced level in reading and math, which paints a disturbing picture for economically disadvantaged students. Education is the primary means for citizens to pull themselves out of the economic situations into which they were born, improve their quality of life, and contribute to society in a meaningful way. With more than 80% of these students graduating below proficiency in essential academic areas, they have limited access to higher education and well-paying jobs. The wealth gap in this country remains intractable and, worse, continues to widen.[14, 15]

The response of many people might be that children of color or those living in poverty must be less capable than others. This kind of thinking has a long and unpleasant history in our country, which can be traced back to the eugenics movement and the misapplication of Darwin's evolutionary theory to justify unfair social practice.[16-18]

During this unfortunate period in our history, which continues to influence many people's perspectives on race today, eugenic arguments were put forth that certain races are genetically inferior to others. The inequitable social conditions inflicted upon people of color have been falsely justified by their supposed genetic inferiority. Not a shred of scientific evidence exists to support these claims. Conversely, much scientific evidence indicates that differences in achievement are due to social inequity, lack of educational opportunity, restricted access to enrichment activities, and an overall lack of resources.[8, 14, 19]

Impoverished learners are the clearest indicator of the ineffectiveness of our educational system. Such learners cannot afford expensive tutoring services, test prep programs, or other educational supplements the way affluent students can. The higher proficiency rates obtained by affluent students can be accounted for in terms of their access to resources *outside* the school environment. Contrary to popular belief, affluent schools don't produce higher proficiency rates because of better instruction. Affluent schools produce higher proficiency rates because their students can access outside resources that supplement school instruction. For a number of reasons, parents living in poverty can't enrich their children's lives in the same ways that affluent parents can. The education of these kids depends almost entirely on what their schools provide. The NAEP data clearly indicate that their schools aren't providing them with very much.

Behavioral science and the Technology of Teaching lead to profound learning gains with every type of student, even those born into poverty. The largest federally funded study of educational methods ever conducted in America involved impoverished learners who qualified for Head Start, an educational initiative aimed at improving the academic achievement of low-income students.[8] That study demonstrated that behaviorally based methods significantly outperformed all other methods and produced dramatic gains in academic achievement with low-income students.

The learning process is the same regardless of age, gender, race, socioeconomic status, or classification. We learn through a very specific process: the repeated reinforcement of our behavior over time until it becomes neurologically permanent. All children learn this way. Unfortunately, for various reasons, children born into poverty may have fewer opportunities to explicitly practice essential skills, and more important, have those explicit practices reinforced. It is a lack of effective learning opportunities that explains the differences in academic achievement between impoverished and affluent students, not some inherent difference in aptitude or ability.

The Systemic Failure of Our Schools Is Often Medicalized

The number of students classified as learning disabled (LD) has exponentially increased since the emergence of this classification in the 1950s.[20, 21] The number of children born with an actual neurological impairment make up less than 1% of the population; however, current epidemiological data indicate that approximately 20% of schoolchildren currently receive LD classifications.[21, 22] This should come as no surprise with respect to the state of American education as a whole. If 60% or more of the general population of school children graduate below proficiency in all academic subjects, how can we be shocked to discover that a significant percentage of these failures are being medicalized? By medicalized I mean that systemic academic failure is frequently attributed to neurological disorders. Not much empirical evidence exists to support this widely held assumption.

More than 90% of students classified as LD graduate below proficiency in science and math, and only slightly less than 90% graduate below proficiency in reading. These data translate to 10% or less of LD students graduating at the proficient level. The Individuals with Disabilities Act was passed as a means of ensuring that disabled students receive an equal and effective education.[23] Students classified as LD gain access to special education services and various accom-modations that are supposed to enable those students to become effec-tively educated despite their "disabilities." However, it is quite clear from the NAEP data that, like the education non-classified students receive, special education services are profoundly ineffective for an overwhelming majority of students classified as LD.

Also shocking is the fact that minority and low-income students perform as poorly as those classified as LD. Of course, a greater per-centage of minority and low-income students are classified as LD, which also represents a troubling trend.[14] When academic failures are medicalized, educators and the educational system as a whole are absolved of responsibility for educating them. The causes for academic failure and social inequity are attributed to characteristics of the individual rather than to ineffective practices, institutional-ized racism or classism, and social factors impacting minority and impoverished kids. As a result, the system remains unchecked and unchanged.

As I have previously stated, the learning process is the same for all students. Permanent learning is produced by the repeated, reinforced practice of skills over time. Unfortunately, schools are not designed this way. Thus, students are pushed ahead to higher level skills before they have mastered the prerequisite skills. Moreover, many students practice the wrong thing, and get really good at behaviors that actu-ally interfere with learning effective skills. Remember Alex and his word-guessing habit? Alex got really good at guessing words. Unfor-tunately, guessing words interfered with reading words correctly, and he was diagnosed with dyslexia as a result. Students become classified as LD because of a failure to master essential skills and because they often develop bad habits that get in the way of their learning. The way schools are designed lead to these tragic outcomes, but because failure to learn is attributed to problems inherent to the student, these ineffec-tive traditions and practices continue.

Male and Female Students Are Being Equally Failed

When NAEP scores are evaluated according to gender, there are some modest differences. Females are being more significantly failed than males in math and science, with close to 80% of female students graduating below proficiency in math and over 80% graduating below proficiency in science. However, male students are certainly not dominating in math and science either, with more than 70% graduating below proficiency in math and science. Female students have a slight edge in reading with less than 60% graduating below proficiency, whereas over 60% of male students graduate below proficiency in reading.

When results are evaluated in terms of the proficient and advanced levels, the state of affairs is profoundly alarming regardless of gender. Less than 10% of graduating students achieve the advanced level in any academic area. Moreover, less than 30% of male and female students achieve proficiency in math and science. A little more than 30% of graduating females achieve proficiency in reading and a little less than 30% of graduating males achieve proficiency in reading. A gender gap still exists in this country, with males outperforming females in math and science and females outperforming males in reading. However, this gap is less cause for alarm than the general pattern of failure across academic domains regardless of gender. In other words, a majority of both male and female students are failing to acquire minimum proficiency in essential academic areas upon completion of their high school education.

Gender does not dictate how the learning process occurs. Lack of proficiency in certain academic areas is not explained by a person's gender. Lack of proficiency is explained by their individual learning histories and subsequent failure to master essential skills. Females may be more inclined to engage in reading activities, and males may be more inclined to engage in activities relating to science and math. However, these inclinations are culturally constructed. Girls are encouraged to engage in activities that seem more "feminine," and boys are encouraged to engage in those that appear more "masculine." However, behavioral science and the Technology of Teaching leads to the mastery of essential academic skills regardless of gender or preexisting preferences for specific activities.

Learning environments can be effectively designed so that males and females acquire mastery in *all* academic subjects, not just those subjects that our culture pushes them toward. Both female and male students have the right to master skills in all subjects so that they can make an actual choice regarding the careers they wish to pursue. Choosing to pursue a career simply due to lack of proficiency in other fields isn't a real choice—it's a forced choice. With behavioral science and the Technology of Teaching, students master essential academic skills in all subjects, which leads to the discovery of their true preferences.

Only a Small Percentage of Students Achieve Advanced Levels

It will come as no surprise that Asian students outperform all other groups, but not by as significant a margin as one might expect. Even with the top performing ethnic groups, less than 40% graduate at the proficient level in math, reading, and science. Even more alarming is the fact that only 10% or less of the high performing groups score at the advanced level, with performance at the advanced level in science the lowest of all the academic domains.[1]

Clearly, no group is dominating. No group is acquiring the kind of accelerated academic preparedness that will enable them to succeed at the college level. In fact, over 75% of entering college freshman require remedial classes in reading, math, and writing.[24] Our educational system is failing everyone, with some groups being more tragically failed than others.

The widely held belief is that expert performers are *born*. In other words, inherent characteristics of learners, like talent, aptitude, and intelligence, are believed to explain why some students achieve high levels of expertise in academic areas. However, no scientific evidence exists that supports this belief. In contrast, scientific evidence actually points to expertise being the result of a very specific type of training.[25] Behavioral science and the Technology of Teaching lead to the design of teaching practices that produce experts. My organization has been producing expert performers for over 20 years. We design learning environments that lead to the achievement of expertise in academic areas. Our performers didn't become experts because of inherent talent or aptitude. They became experts as a result of training based in behavioral science and the Technology of Teaching.

Type of School Attended Does Not Significantly Impact Achievement

Privatization and school choice remain key political issues at the center of the debate regarding school reform.[26-28] In the early 1990s, the charter school movement arose based on the idea that parents should have the right to choose the school their children attend, and the belief that if the school system resembled the free marketplace, competition for public funds would naturally lead to the improvement of educational practices. However, the most recent NAEP data indicate that there are virtually no differences in educational outcomes for students who attend public versus charter schools. In fact, public schools actually outperformed charter schools in both math and reading on the most recent NAEP. Contrary to popular belief, charter schools are not producing better outcomes despite the consistent efforts made to offer charter schools as an effective alternative to public schools. However, there are differences in test scores for students enrolled in private Catholic schools.

The private Catholic schools that participated in the 2019 NAEP outperformed public and charter schools in reading and math. However, these private Catholic schools also failed to produce proficiency with a majority of their students. Less than 50% of 8th graders enrolled in private Catholic schools achieved proficient levels in reading and math on the 2019 NAEP. A little more than 10% of Catholic school students achieved the advanced level in math and less than 10% of Catholic school students achieved the advanced level in reading. Although the percent of students performing at proficient and advanced levels did exceed those of public and charter schools, these percentages still failed to demonstrate superior academic outcomes with a majority of students enrolled, which should be expected of an expensive private education.

The vast majority of school reform efforts have involved arguments in favor of privatization and school choice. These issues remain central themes in the political debate regarding school reform. However, the data on this issue are clear. Educational practices in this country are widely ineffective regardless of whether they are occurring in public, charter, or private Catholic school settings. A majority of American students fail to achieve proficiency in academic subjects regardless of the type of school they attend.

Public, charter, and private Catholic school settings produce similarly mediocre outcomes because the way these schools are designed, and the teaching practices used, are largely the same. Though the setting and types of students enrolled may differ, the way students are educated is the same. The improved outcomes produced with students in private Catholic schools can be widely attributed to the fact that those schools are primarily attended by students whose parents can supplement their education with resources outside of the school environment. But the teaching practices used across all of these schools are the same. Later in the book, we'll see what teaching practices guided by behavioral science and the Technology of Teaching entail, and why such practices consistently produce superior academic outcomes with all students.

American Schools Have Never Produced Proficiency for a Majority of Students

As I mentioned previously, our country's complacency about the grim reality of our educational system largely stems from the fact that this crisis is not new.[4, 29, 30] Figures 1 and 2 illustrate average NAEP scores for reading and math obtained with 12th graders since its inception during the 1970s.[1]

These figures reflect that there have been no significant gains in academic achievement since the dawn of the NAEP. For close to 50 years, a majority of graduating students have scored well below proficient levels in essential academic areas. These same historical trends in achievement hold true for 4th and 8th grade students. I have included figures reflecting the long-term trends for 4th and 8th grade

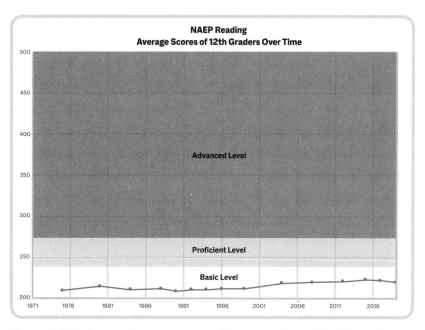

Figure 1. This figure reflects average reading scores obtained by 12th graders on the NAEP from 1978 to 2015. The figure is divided to reflect cutoff score ranges for the basic, proficient, and advanced levels.

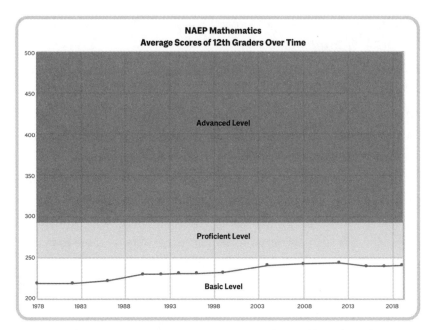

Figure 2. This figure reflects average math scores obtained by 12th graders on the NAEP from 1978 to 2015. The figure is divided to reflect cutoff score ranges for the basic, proficient, and advanced levels.

students in the appendix for this chapter. Although gains in reading and math have been achieved with 4th and 8th graders over time, these gains still failed to produce average NAEP scores at the proficient level, and no significant gains have been produced with 4th and 8th grade students in the last decade. Further, as the long-term trends for 12th graders indicate, any gains in achievement made with 4th and 8th graders are essentially lost by 12th grade. Graduating students in America are no better off today than they were almost five decades ago.

Moreover, the first broad-scale evaluation of educational outcomes was conducted in 1948, and the results of that initial study were no different from all that have followed it.[4] For more than 80 years, an overwhelming majority of students have failed to acquire proficiency in essential academic areas. This failure continued even during the era of No Child Left Behind (NCLB), when heavy policy reforms regarding mandatory statewide testing were implemented, and greater account-ability was required of schools regarding student achievement.[31]

The NAEP data clearly indicate that top-down educational reform efforts like NCLB do not result in improved student achievement. Top-down reform efforts involve changes made at the level of policy, such as increasing or reallocating school funds, mandating testing, provid-ing school choice, increasing school accountability, and expanding administrative oversight. However, it is clear that no such effort has resulted in the effective education of a majority of our nation's chil-dren. As stated in the introduction, not a single reform effort through-out the history of our educational system has resulted in a majority of American students being effectively educated. No reform effort has significantly improved academic achievement because none of these efforts has involved reform of the teaching practices themselves.

PROGRAM OF INTERNATIONAL STUDENT ASSESSMENT (PISA)

Although I wrote this book with reference to the crisis in American education, the current state of affairs reflects a global issue. As I will show in the section that follows, American students also struggle to compete on international assessments of academic achievement; how-ever, educational systems around the globe also produce mediocre outcomes. Although many countries do outperform the United States, none achieve high levels of academic expertise with a majority of stu-dents because no country in the world designs its teaching practices according to behavioral science and the Technology of Teaching.

The results of the most recent PISA, or Program of International Stu-dent Assessment, indicate that out of over 70 industrialized countries, the United States ranks 13th in reading, 18th in science, and 37th in math.[32] American students scored well below the international average with respect to math, and only slightly above average for reading and science. For the 2015 PISA, the U.S. rankings were much worse across all academic domains. In 2015, the United States ranked 24th in reading, 25th in science, and 40th in math. Our increased rankings might lead one to think that American students made significant improvements from 2015 to 2018. Unfortunately, our increased rankings do not reflect improvements in our achievement scores but rather the dramatic decreases in achievement across many other countries. For those countries that scored better than the United States on the 2015 PISA, 19 countries decreased in their reading scores, 21 countries decreased in their science scores, and 18 countries decreased in their math scores on the 2018 PISA. American achievement scores showed relatively no change from 2015 to 2018; however, the dramatic decreases in academic achievement in many countries resulted in our improved rankings.

No single country is knocking the cover off the ball in terms of their PISA scores. Although BSJZ-China (Beijing, Shanghai, Jiangsu, and Zhejiang) and Singapore typically outperform everyone else, clarification of what these scores mean is warranted. The subdomains of the PISA test typically involve between six and seven levels of proficiency, with Levels 5 through 7 indicating top performers and Levels 1 and 2 indicating low performers. Levels 3 and 4 reflect somewhat average levels of competence.

Even as the top performing countries, average scores for BSJZ-China did not exceed Level 4 across all domains, and Singapore did not exceed Level 3 for science and reading or Level 4 for math. Similarly, the United States did not exceed Level 3 for reading and science and did not exceed Level 2 for math. In other words, although scoring at the higher end of the range for Level 3, Singaporean students scored in the same average levels for science and reading as students in the United States. However, Singapore outperformed the United States by two levels in math. BSJZ-China outperformed the United States by one level in reading and science and by two levels in math.

Students in the top-performing Asian countries spend significantly more time on schoolwork and test preparation than American students.[33-35] There have been numerous reports of the grueling conditions in which these students must work — attending school from very early in the morning until six or seven each night only to move to a private test-preparation center until ten or eleven p.m. Many students do not return home until after ten each night, when they still must complete homework and possibly practice their musical instruments. These schedules hardly seem ideal. Students in these top performing countries have little time to just be kids. There have been reports of such students being so sleep-deprived that teachers regularly use plush toys attached to a string at the end of a stick to wake them in class by tapping them on the head.[33] Yet even with these grueling schedules, a majority of them do not score at the highest levels of proficiency. Although such countries typically outperform us, one must question if the modest gain is worth the sacrifice these students and families must make.

The take-home point is that no country in the world achieved average PISA scores above the Level 4 range.[32] Moreover, even in the top performing countries, only a small minority of students are able to perform at the highest levels. In the United States, only 9% of students performed at the highest level in science, only 8% of students performed at the highest level in math, and only 14% achieved the highest level in reading.[32] These percentages are much smaller than some of the higher performing countries, but even in those countries, a majority of students fail to achieve the highest levels. Education around the globe is producing mediocre performances with a majority of students. The mediocrity of American students appears more alarming because of our general standing as the superpower in the world and the amount of resources we invest in education.

Out of all countries included in the PISA outcomes, only four countries spend more than the United States per student: Luxembourg,

Norway, Austria, and Singapore.[32] The United States spends approximately $100,000 per student, from the age of 6 years old at the start of their primary education to 15 years old when they sit for the PISA test. We spend 20% more per student than Canada and Germany and twice as much per student as Estonia, all of which performed better than we did on the most recent PISA test.[32]

These results do not reflect well on our very expensive educational system. In other words, we are getting a pretty poor return on our investment. Research shows a 1:1 correlation between scores on the PISA and a nation's long-term economic growth.[33] We should all be concerned with the direction our economy is headed based on our abysmal PISA scores. The educational crisis in this country has the possibility of impacting all of us and should be a major concern for every American citizen.

As I have mentioned, no country in the world designs its educational practices according to behavioral science and the Technology of Teaching. Training of teachers in countries like Finland has been vastly improved by dismantling traditional colleges of education in favor of focused training in a specific discipline followed by an apprenticeship with a master teacher.[33] However, Finnish teachers are still not trained in the science of learning. On the most recent PISA, Finland outperformed the United States across all domains, and it is clear that improvements in their PISA scores are correlated with the reform of their teacher training programs.[32] However, even with these improvements, the majority of Finnish students score below the highest levels of proficiency, like students in other top-performing countries.

As I will argue throughout the remainder of this book, traditional teaching practices are highly ineffective and inefficient because they are based on theories and beliefs rather than science. Educational systems around the globe exist as ideological institutions not pragmatic ones. Pragmatic institutions are those that evolve over time through science, where ineffective practices are discarded as more effective ones are systematically identified. Medicine, engineering, and agriculture are examples of pragmatic institutions where remarkable advances have been made through the scientific process. However, these kinds of advances have never been made with respect to education. Education is as ineffective and inefficient today as it was a century ago. Although developed countries around the world continue to value and invest in education, this investment is largely wasted on a profoundly ineffective and inefficient system guided by ideology rather than science.

We have a global need for highly educated individuals capable of solving the many complex problems facing the human race. Although separated by geography, we are connected as a species and we all face the same threats to our existence. We all desire survival and advancement, both of which require a highly educated world populace. We have a global educational crisis, not just an American one, and instruction guided by behavioral science can provide us with its solution.

EDUCATION REQUIRES REFORM FROM THE BOTTOM UP

Let's step back to the 2019 NAEP press conference, which revealed that a majority of teachers and members of the establishment fundamentally *believe* that a shortage of school supplies is a major factor impeding teachers' abilities to teach effectively. It makes perfect sense that teachers shouldn't have to use their own money to purchase the materials needed for their classrooms and that all students should have the necessary materials. Basic material resources are required in education and schools should be properly funded to ensure that they are available. But material resources and effective teaching practices are two very different things. With training in behavioral science, you could effectively teach a child to read with a pencil and paper if you had to. Fancy materials don't lead to better learning outcomes—effective teaching practices lead to better learning outcomes.

The bottom line is, learners fail because of ineffective teaching practices. Without effective teaching practices, educational outcomes cannot possibly improve. No amount of policy reform will ever change the fact that the way teachers teach fundamentally does not work. Our educational system requires reform from the bottom up. Without implementation of instruction designed from the science of human learning, none of the top-down policy reform efforts have any chance of effectiveness. The problem stems from the way teachers are teaching, and more important, the way teachers are being trained to teach. No amount of money or administrative oversight can improve a system that fundamentally does not work at its very core. To improve education, teaching practices must improve, and to improve teaching practices, teacher training must improve. We must redesign our educational system from the ground up starting with how teachers are trained to teach in the first place.

2

THE ESTABLISHMENTS

*"Concerning the central fact of educational failure there is
relatively slight dispute; and the failure itself underlines one
of the paradoxes of American life: that in a society so passionately
intent upon education, the yield of our educational system
has been such a constant disappointment."*
—RICHARD HOFSTADTER[36]

When my son, Jack, was four years old, he started preschool. However, preschool didn't mark the beginning of his formal education, as he had already been enrolled at Fit Learning for two years at that point. Jack actually served as the catalyst for the development of our accelerated learning program for very young learners. By the time he came into the world, I had witnessed far too many children like Alex, already set up for academic failure by first grade. In other words, their early childhood educations were not sufficiently preparing them to succeed in primary school.

So I developed a program at Fit Learning for Jack to strengthen his "learning to learn" skills, like following instructions and sitting for extended periods of time. We also strengthened his language skills and ability to understand more abstract concepts, as well as early literacy skills like identifying letter names and sounds. By the time Jack started preschool, he had a strong foundation in early cognitive and academic skills.

But Jack was also a classic jokester. Making people laugh was, and remains, a powerfully reinforcing experience for Jack, which can be traced back to his first year of life. This preference was well established by his older sister, Emma, who was five when Jack was born. The minute Jack came into the world, Emma was on a mission to make him laugh, and she was profoundly successful. Those early years with my kids were hilarious. I can still hear the two of them laughing incessantly in every room of the house, each one taking turns doing something silly, which resulted in the other laughing until one or both of them got the hiccups. Nick and I aren't innocent in this aspect of his development either. We both enjoy a good laugh and have definitely reinforced Jack's hilarious antics throughout his life. We would explicitly tell him not to put his peas in his yogurt and then say "Ew, gross!" very loudly and laugh hysterically when, of course, he put his peas in the yogurt immediately after being told not to. By the time Jack started preschool, he had been well trained in the art of testing boundaries and making people laugh.

It wasn't long into the school year when Nick and I were called in for a dreaded parent-teacher meeting where we were informed that his teacher had concerns regarding his development. She informed us that when Jack entered the classroom each morning, he wasn't "signing in" properly. Now, remember that my son was four years old at this point. Regardless, he was expected to stop by the sign-in sheet on his way into the classroom and write his name. Well, Jack wasn't too keen on this requirement, so instead of writing his name—which he had already learned how to do quite well at Fit Learning—Jack would quickly scribble something so he could get on with the business of playing with his pals. We were also informed that Jack wouldn't come to circle time when called but would remain in whatever part of the classroom he happened to be playing. Finally, we were told that when the teacher asked Jack to identify his letters—which he had already mastered at Fit Learning—he would identify every letter as "p." Side note: Potty humor has always been a favorite in our household, so notice that the letter name he chose also resembles the word for that thing people do in the bathroom that Jack found pretty hilarious at that age.

Jack's teacher recommended that we have him evaluated for a developmental disability. From her perspective, the fact that he wasn't properly "signing in" to class, wasn't coming to circle time when called, and identified all of his letters as "p" meant that there must be something seriously *wrong* with him. I'm sure you can imagine how Nick and I responded to this recommendation. First, we asked the teacher what she did when Jack failed to do these things. She looked at us blankly and said that she would repeat her instruction, but if he didn't respond after her second request she would let him continue what he was doing because apparently he wasn't "ready" to do whatever she had asked him to do. Nick and I informed her that if she waited for Jack to be ready to do anything other than play, she would be waiting for a very long time.

Within five minutes of that interaction, the school principal, school psychologist, and director of early childhood education were in that meeting with us. When we vehemently disagreed with the teacher's assessment of the situation, it set off a schoolwide panic. So we took that opportunity to create some distinctions for them—uncover their blind spots if you will—regarding a different interpretation of our son's behavior in her classroom.

By the end of the meeting, the team had agreed to implement a "star chart" with him, where he earned a star sticker on a chart each time he properly signed in, came to circle time when asked, and identified his letters correctly. Jack would bring his star chart home with him at the end of the day, and each star he had earned could be exchanged for treats or privileges at home. Within three days of implementing this intervention in the classroom, Jack never missed earning a star sticker. We were also able to quickly remove this earning system, and eventually Jack was engaging properly in the classroom on his own without these external incentives. Problem solved.

Now imagine if I had been a parent without my knowledge and experience. Imagine if I had been a parent who had blind spots about the real reasons my child was failing to succeed in the classroom. I likely would have followed the teacher's recommendation and had my child evaluated for a disability of some sort. Based on my child's antics in the classroom, it is highly likely that those same antics would have shown up during an outside evaluation, and it's likely that my child would have been diagnosed with a developmental disorder or learning disability. But, as I hope I have made clear, Jack wasn't disabled at all. Quite the contrary, my son had learned how to game the system. He didn't have to take the time to sign his name or leave a fun activity to come to boring circle time because, when he didn't do what his teacher asked, she left him alone and he got to continue doing what he wanted. He also found it pretty hilarious to name each letter as "p."

Rather than a simple solution that changed the course of Jack's preschool year, that meeting could have resulted in a lifelong classification. The phrase "making a mountain out of a molehill" perfectly captures the recommendations frequently made by members of the establishments. More often than not, classroom failure has a simple explanation and a simple solution—both of which involve modifying a student's learning environment in some way. However, this pragmatic approach rarely occurs in education. When students struggle in the classroom, members of the establishments look for explanations *outside* of the classroom rather than focusing on the environment in which the problem is occurring. Having Jack evaluated for a disability would have led to special services being provided by another member of the establishments outside of the environment in which those problems arose.

Moreover, Jack was one of the lucky ones, with parents who provided him with enrichment outside of the school environment. Jack showed up to preschool with a lot of prerequisite skills already mastered. His issues in the classroom were purely motivational. He had the skills, but he just wasn't using them. However, many children must actually learn and master skills in the classroom. Jack's preschool teacher was providing him with opportunities to perform certain skills, but those opportunities won't work very well for a child who hasn't learned whatever skill is required. Children need to learn and master skills in the classroom, not just be provided with the opportunity to perform them. Unfortunately, many children never effectively learn and master these kinds of basic skills in the classroom, because the way schools are designed and the way teachers are trained fundamentally doesn't work.

Whom can we blame for this sorry state of affairs? That's the classic human response, right? When something goes wrong, the first thing we do is look for someone or something to blame. I know that I sound quite blamey at this point. And I am. I am blaming the establishments. But let's be clear that by establishments I am not referring to one specific person or even a set of people. These various establishments represent historical systems of beliefs, traditions, practices, and rules that almost seem like a real living, breathing organism. But the establishments are not really alive. Although they do seem to take on a life of their own to some degree, in actuality they are not living entities, which is exactly what makes establishments so dangerous and so difficult to change. Who is in charge of these establishments? Whom can we blame? Whom can we remove from power? Whom can we attack? Whom can we protest against? Establishments lead us to ask these kinds of questions.

However, I am going to offer that, sadly, *we* are the establishments I am referring to. Establishments are kept alive, fed, and nurtured by us—the members of society who go along with and actually encourage everything that the establishments represent. Unfortunately, we are the reason our educational system fails so many children. Of course, none of this is intentional. Most of us don't intentionally go along with traditions and practices that marginalize and suppress people or prevent progress. We tend to go along with establishments because they reflect our own beliefs. The establishments provide us with agreement or a way to avoid being responsible or having to tackle things that are difficult and make us uncomfortable. In the long run, all we want as human beings is to live our lives in happiness, avoid discomfort, keep ourselves and our loved ones safe, gain access to resources that improve our quality of life, and ensure our own survival. We really are quite selfish, we humans.

If we all are a part of these establishments, we have to ask ourselves, are we willing to change? Are we willing to get a little uncomfortable as we give up our addiction to certain beliefs, traditions, and myths that prevent us from making progress? Are we willing to say *time's up* to the establishments? Because we will be saying that to ourselves. Are we ready to say that our own time is up? Are we brave enough to declare that time is up on our own entrenched beliefs, which give rise to the promulgation of establishments, and ultimately, the continuation of ineffective educational practices? Let's explore some of these establishments at work and perhaps determine what we can do about them.

THE EDUCATIONAL ESTABLISHMENT

The Rise of Compulsory Schooling

For starters, the educational establishment reflects the ideology of *progressive* education, and has since the turn of the 20th century.[5, 37]

During the mid-1800s, with the increasing population, influx of immigrants, and the industrial revolution, came the need for systematic and organized education. During this period, philosophers, scientists, and scholars began calling for education as a means of social reform. Horace Mann was the first prominent reformer of the time to call for a nationwide public education system.[38, 39] Mann believed that education was the means of upholding our democratic ideals and ensuring the betterment of all citizens. John Dewey also began advocating for education as a means of social reform, and his writings largely gave rise to the progressive education movement in America.[40-43] Before Mann and Dewey, education was highly formal, available mainly to the privileged, heavily focused on academic training, and largely based on authoritative control and rote recitation.[5]

Progressive education, then, was part of a shift in the zeitgeist in America that began gaining momentum toward the end of the 19th century as a result of vast cultural changes. The movement was originally spawned from the notion that our nation needed to make progress, to evolve beyond the purely intellectual purposes of education to meet the demands of our modernizing society. With the rise of compulsory public education, schools were filled with students from diverse backgrounds. No longer was schooling available only to the privileged few. Suddenly, heterogeneous groups of youngsters were *required* to attend school. How was the nation to deal with the issue of motivating large groups of youngsters without resorting to punitive and authoritarian methods Americans tended to instinctively reject?

In this sense, progressive education was born from humanitarian values. Social activists from all walks of life joined in the effort to rethink and reshape education in America. Due to rapid urbanization, cities had become overcrowded, impoverished places with many families living in squalor. Urban activists viewed education as a means of upward mobility for poor, immigrant families in search of the American dream. Businessmen of the time (and they were mainly *men* at that point) viewed education as the means to advance capitalist ideals and prepare our youth for successful entry into the workforce. Farmers viewed education as a means of providing children with preparation for a life in agriculture; with our increasing population, ensuring the survival and advancement of the farming industry was of great importance. Political idealists viewed education as a means of instilling moral values and democratic ideals into the hearts and minds of our country's youth to ensure the survival and advancement of our democracy, particularly in the face of increasing threats abroad. The turn of the 20th century was an exciting time for the United States, and resulted in a complete reform of its educational system.

By 1917, the National Education Association had appointed a committee of professional educators charged with the task of reorganizing secondary education. Social reformers, businessmen, farmers, and political idealists came together in a national dialogue calling for a total revamping of the purposes of education and what the school curriculum should entail, and the professional educators responded. The commission released a report entitled "The Cardinal Principles," and it would forever alter the ideological goals of education.[44]

The commission recommended shifting the goal of schooling away from a traditional liberal education that emphasized intellectual training in academic subjects toward a greater emphasis on vocational training, home economics, the development of morals and values, and the general adjustment of the whole child to life as a productive member of society. This led to schools playing a greater role in areas typically dominated by the family, church, and community.[35] The notion was that a well-rounded education would be more likely to keep youngsters interested in school and increase the likelihood that they would complete their education. At the time, a majority of the nation's youth left school well before starting high school. In order to ensure the advancement of our nation, the complete education of our youth was of paramount concern.

As the content of the curriculum was being dramatically altered, so were the teaching methods. Near the turn of the 20th century, progressive school models were being developed and tested throughout the country.[5] These models involved an eclectic mix of methods in which schools attempted to address development of the "whole child." Classes were student directed, exploratory, and experiential, and children learned by doing rather than through lecture and recitation. Educators began taking children on field trips around the community to study geography, civics, science, agriculture, and mathematics. Many such schools did away with grades or evaluations of any sort. The focus was on a more organic experience intended to encourage play, physical activity, creativity, and discovery. Educators involved in such schools reported highly positive results, which piqued the interests of journalists, politicians, and educators from every corner of the nation, who often visited the programs to see this revolution in education for themselves. This led to more public schools across the country adopting bits and pieces of the progressive approach. By the 1920s, the traditional authoritarian, recitation models had all but disappeared.

The reformation of our nation's schools during the early 20th century was based purely on ideology. The efforts were centered on *beliefs* about what children should learn and how they should learn it. The experimental programs put forth by progressive educators were not evaluated from a scientific perspective. The developers of such programs were not scientists at all. They were an eclectic mix of professional educators, teachers, parents, and educational philosophers who had various opinions about how children learn and how schools should be designed.

Moreover, the evaluations of these programs were done subjectively, based on the opinions of those who had developed them and the interpretations of those who visited them. Thus, the success of such programs was determined *ideologically*. In other words, if schools reflected the progressive beliefs of educators, then those schools were viewed as successful. No formal methods to obtain objective achievement data with students existed at the time. Educational practices were not evaluated pragmatically or in terms of their effectiveness for producing learning and mastery of skills and content; they were evaluated only ideologically. Again, the ideas of these reformers stemmed from humanitarian values that were part of an agenda of change put forth by the culture at large. They held that children should enjoy school, be protected from punitive methods of authoritative control, and that learning should involve more than memorization and recitation of facts. All of these beliefs reflect values that continue to be shared by our culture today.

Normal Schools and the History of Teacher Training

With the growing need for mass education, so too came the growing need for teachers and for professional schools in which to train them.[6] Prior to the establishment of formal colleges of education, teachers were predominantly untrained and uneducated. Teaching was more of a trade than a profession. Over time the push to professionalize the job of teachers led to the development of the first normal schools, which were ultimately vocational schools. These normal schools for teachers became the heart of the progressive education movement, with many establishing their own experimental schools aimed at testing teaching methods based on progressive ideologies. Eventually these independent vocational training schools began to merge with colleges and universities, so that teachers began receiving formal degrees and professional credentials in the form of teaching certificates and licenses.

Although these normal schools became part of already existing liberal arts institutions, they were largely separate entities inside those institutions.[6] Colleges of education began and have ultimately remained isolated from the scholarly activities occurring within the institutions that house them. Teacher training programs were, and continue to be, developed solely by professional educators—those individuals who maintain that what children should learn and how they should learn it are ideological matters. In other words, professional educators do not view their field from a scientific perspective, but rather from a philosophical one. Colleges of education arose during the rise of progressivism in this country where *beliefs* regarding how education could improve our nation were the driving force behind the design of curriculum as well as the methods used to teach it.

Today, most teachers are trained by professional educators in colleges of education, which continue to be concerned with ideological issues regarding education. A majority of the coursework teachers are required to take involves *theories* about learning, teaching methods, child development, self-concept and self-esteem, ethics, curriculum content, and the ideological goals of education. More often than not, when it comes to the academic subjects, teachers take pedagogical versions of these courses.[4] Simply put, professional educators present their own versions of history, geography, the natural sciences, civics, mathematics, and English. Courses in literacy reflect various theories regarding how children learn to read and how reading instruction should occur. Undergraduate education majors rarely take courses from scholars in the specific disciplines that they will ultimately be required to teach; during their undergraduate and graduate training in education, teachers are effectively isolated from scholarly activities occurring inside the liberal arts institutions that they are attending.

The educational establishment arose in response to a shift in the zeitgeist in American culture. It came to fruition as a response to our nation's demands regarding what education should entail. The educational establishment ultimately reflects the beliefs and values of American culture, of which *we are all a part*. Unfortunately, it has also evolved as an ideological entity largely isolated from the intellectual and scholarly activities of other disciplines. With that isolation has come an entrenched dogmatism regarding what should be taught and how it should be taught. Without training in science and its philosophical underpinnings, educators have neither the motivation nor the means of evaluating the effectiveness of their practices from a scientific perspective. As with religious ideology, institutions based solely on *belief* fundamentally cannot evolve because evolution ultimately stems from scientific inquiry. Ideology cannot be proven or disproven—it is purely a matter of faith. You either believe it or you don't. The litmus test in education simply entails a consideration of whether teaching practices reflect what the establishment believes those teaching practices should be. Effectiveness and outcome are not the concern of ideological institutions; they are the concerns of pragmatic ones.

THE PSYCHOLOGICAL ESTABLISHMENT

Theories of Child Development

The field of psychology also experienced a shift in the zeitgeist during the turn of the 20th century. There was a growing interest in the scientific understanding of human behavior leading to debates within the field regarding the appropriate subject matter of psychology and the methods best fit to study it.[45, 46]

Psychological theories about child development exerted great influence over the educational reform efforts of the early 20th century, and still dominate educational practices.[5] Developmental theorists set about to understand the general growth and development of children from a psychological perspective. This work was theoretical in nature and was conducted via observation, where consistent patterns of behavior throughout childhood were described and classified into various stages of development.[47-58] A leap was then made to offering stages as explanations for why children behave the way they do, and these theories are still prominent in our culture. The "terrible twos" is a prime example of the entrenched cultural belief that age, or developmental stage, is the cause of the notorious tantrums of toddlers.

Again, these now entrenched ideologies that dominate our culture arose from theories rather than the methods of natural science.[47, 59–63] Developmental theory entails the classic error of *correlation* being confused with *causation*. Simply because phenomena reliably co-occur does not confirm a causal relationship between those phenomena. That error is a classic demonstration of pseudoscience being mistaken for actual science.[64]

The Rise of Psychological Testing

Beyond theories regarding child development, the branch of psychology focused on the study of cognition or mental events has exerted the greatest influence in education. The assertion is that the realm of cognitive activity sets human beings apart from other animals.[45] Reasoning, thinking, feeling, problem-solving, and emoting are all uniquely human activities and naturally, psychology should focus on a scientific understanding of the activities that essentially make us human. From the cognitive perspective, behavior is just a byproduct of the essence of humanity—mental life. Mental activity is seen as separate and, ultimately, more important than the actual behavior of human beings.

At the turn of the 20th century, the advancement of psychological testing eventually influenced the establishment of educational psychology as a formal field of study and the formal inculcation of the psychological establishment as part of the educational establishment.[65–72] The result of that effort culminated in the 1920s with the introduction into schools of intelligence and aptitude testing, which were already used by the military as a means of evaluating men to determine their fitness to serve.[5] The psychological testing movement matched the ideology of the greater culture at the time, which continues to this day. Since the dawn of civilization, humans have been seeking *the truth*. Humans have been on a quest to understand the meaning of life. Why are we here? Why do we do the things we do? Historically, answers to such questions have been provided by religion. We are here because

God created the universe. We do the things we do because God granted us life and with it a soul that guides and directs us. The soul is what ultimately makes us human. Thus, the causes of human behavior are presumed to be metaphysical. From this perspective, to understand life is to understand its essence, which is the metaphysical aspect of existence.

But then a major branch of psychology got into the business of trying to make the metaphysical the subject of scientific study. The first thing required for scientific analysis is measurement; to understand anything from a scientific point of view, one must be able to measure it in some way. Through psychometrics, tests were designed that supposedly allowed the measurement of the inherent, metaphysical aspects of human beings. IQ tests were the first such tests and were purported to measure innate intelligence or ability. The testing movement exploded into a multitude of psychological tests of various sorts that were supposed to measure traits, characteristics, disorders, aptitude, and the like. At last, the unmeasurable was seen to be measurable, and modern psychology as we know it today was born.

THE MEDICAL ESTABLISHMENT

The Disease Model

The psychological testing movement fits nicely into the disease model of medicine. Hence, the medical establishment influenced the psychological establishment. In medicine, doctors *infer* disease from observed symptoms. However, when possible, various tests and procedures are used to verify their inferences and formally diagnose a particular disease. The diagnosis of disease then guides its subsequent treatment. These diseases have been given various names: influenza, strep throat, cancer, etc. However, the name of the disease provides no *explanation* for it. The explanation for the disease lies in the process of infection as it attacks the body and its corresponding treatment is based on a scientific understanding of this process and the variables that disrupt or terminate that process. This model works exceptionally well in medicine, and advancements in modern medicine have led to the improved health and longevity of the human race.

Unfortunately, a pretty big leap is made in applying that model to psychology, where assumed internal pathologies are said to account for a host of psychological problems. This model is the dominant ideology in modern psychology and has greatly influenced the educational establishment. In line with the disease model, modern psychology views behavior as symptomatic of some underlying, inherent cause. Inferences are made regarding the causes of those behaviors. Psychological tests are administered, and inferences are then made as a means of explaining a person's performance on that test. The performance on the test is not of interest to psychologists of this sort. It is the *inferences* made regarding that performance that are paramount. Tests are given, inferences are made based on performance on the test, and a psychological or psychiatric diagnosis is given. The assumed pathology has not been directly measured or observed in any way, unlike in medicine where inferences made from symptoms can be directly verified with blood tests or some other procedure. This same level of verification is not possible with psychological tests because the assumed causes are *hypothetical* in nature. The diagnosis is an inference made about underlying causes for test performance and that inference is given a name, which is seen as explaining the behavior or the test performance.

This practice reflects the *nominal fallacy* or the mistake of assuming that something has been explained by *naming it*.[46] In reality nothing has been explained. Unfortunately, this model appeals to the ideology of the greater culture, where the masses believe that inherent, metaphysical aspects of human beings determine why we do the things we do. These kinds of metaphysical explanations dominate our everyday vernacular. We don't speak publicly due to our *anxiety*. We don't go out because we are *depressed*. We listen to a particular song repeatedly because we are *obsessed* with it. We hate losing because we are *competitive*. We don't play an instrument because we aren't *talented*. We performed well on a test because we are *smart*. We didn't perform well on a test because we are *stupid*. In each of these examples, we are all perfectly comfortable with the idea that naming our behavior explains it. As harmless as this practice appears in everyday life, it is absolutely tragic with respect to education.

As I have previously argued, schools are designed based on beliefs about what children should learn and how they should learn it. Unfortunately, as our NAEP scores indicate, these beliefs have not led to the effective education of a majority of students. The measurable failure of schools was first identified in the early 1940s after the development of academic achievement tests led to the first broad-scale evaluation of educational outcomes.[4] The results of that initial study were no different from the results of those that have followed it. For over 80 years, our nation's schools have consistently failed to produce academic proficiency for a majority of students. But let us remember that the educators who have always been in charge have never been trained as scientists. They were, and remain, ideologues. As a result, after 80 years, teaching practices remain unchanged and a majority of students remain uneducated.

Psychological testing represents the most tragic, large-scale misuse of so-called science in education.[36] When schools began using IQ testing regularly, a majority of students were found to have low IQs and therefore were considered to be largely uneducable. IQ was presumed to be "real," rather than simply a test performance reflective of a child's learning history and opportunities to master specific skills. IQ was mistakenly given causal status and used as an explanation for the academic failures that large-scale evaluations of educational outcomes regularly identified. Rather than considering the possibility that ineffective teaching practices were a possible cause for general academic failure, these failures were, and continue to be, attributed to low IQ or other inherent characteristics of students. The psychological establishment paved the way for this practice to dominate the educational establishment. As I have said, ideological institutions gather evidence to verify their beliefs.

During the rise of the psychological testing movement and its alignment with the disease model of medicine, there were, and continue to be, more pragmatically oriented psychologists committed to the understanding of human behavior as a natural science. I happen to be one of those individuals, and I will more fully introduce you to our group in the next chapter. Of course, not all psychologists agree with the practice of explaining behavior by naming it or assume that behavior has some inherent, metaphysical cause. For this reason, the veracity of psychological testing has been a hotly debated topic since its formal inception in the 1950s.

The Brain Movement

To verify the practice of inferring psychological disorders from performance on psychological tests, the psychological establishment attempted to further align itself with the highly regarded and scientifically validated medical establishment by shifting its focus to the brain. We are absolutely brain obsessed as a culture. You'd think that we are just brains in jars walking around given the priority the brain receives as an explanation for everything we do. As is the case with most ideological institutions based on theory or belief, the psychological establishment set about to gather evidence to verify its theories regarding inherent psychic disorders as the cause for behavior.

These hypothetical disorders were redefined as "inherent neurological dysfunctions."[21] In order to verify their existence, the psychological establishment began conducting brain scans, such as fMRIs, of individuals classified as "normal" and comparing them with scans of individuals who had been classified through psychological testing as having a disorder of some sort, such as "dyslexia." Some of these comparisons did uncover neurological differences, which were then presented as evidence confirming the psychological establishment's theories that dysfunctions in the brain are the cause for the "disorder" that had been previously identified by a psychological test. For example, in the case of dyslexia, the theory regarding neurological dysfunction as the cause of a reading problem was assumed to be verified because the brains of some kids classified as dyslexic showed up differently on a brain scan when compared with the brains of kids not classified in this way.

Again, as with the developmental theories previously described, we have the classic error of correlation being confused with causation. It is assumed that the differences in brain scans are indicative of a causal relation; however, none has been demonstrated. The notion that dysfunction in the brain is the cause of the reading problem remains theoretical. All that has been identified are differences—the causes of those differences remain unknown.

Recently, neuroscience has led to a greater understanding of the neuroplasticity of the brain.[25, 73–81] We now know that the brain adapts and responds as a person behaves in their environment. The brain plays an enormous role in human behavior; however, it is becoming clear that this role is less causal than it is *responsive* and *adaptive*. In other words, we have evolved as a species such that our brains change as a function of how we behave and, more important, what occurs as a function of that behavior as it occurs in the environment.

So it should come as no surprise that poor readers show up differently on brain scans when compared with strong readers. Poor readers behave differently with respect to reading material than strong readers do, and they behave differently because of insufficient training. Neuroscience has made discoveries regarding the impact that *training* has on the establishment of neural pathways and the altering of neurological profiles. Poor readers have failed to learn to read properly because of inadequate training, and as a result, they have different neurological profiles than those learners who have learned to read well. However, their neurological differences are the *result* of the kind of reading training they received, not the *cause* of those differences.

The psychological establishment clings to the notion that our brains push and guide us through life as a causal force that simply unfolds and develops over time, due either to our genetic hardwiring or, even more appealing to the public, to the metaphysical forces inherent in human beings. The idea of the brain as a causal agent appeals to cultural belief. If our behavior has to be caused or controlled by something, let it be our own brains rather than external forces beyond our control. The "brain as cause theory" fits into our beliefs regarding the soul — the brain being viewed as the physical organ that helps our soul translate itself into actions.

Unfortunately, the psychological establishment misrepresents these *correlational* brain scan studies as verification of the existence of inherent neurological dysfunction.[21] The public now believes that learning disabilities and other psychological disorders have been "proven" to be the causes of learning or behavior problems. But nothing has been "proven" at all. Correlations have been identified and misrepresented as causes — another tragic misuse of so-called science by the psychological establishment that has infiltrated the educational establishment.

Now that learning disabilities appear to have been proven by brain scans, attributing academic failure to inherent disorders rather than faulty teaching practices seems justified. Thus, the psychological establishment has given rise to the institutionalization of ineffective educational practices by providing a supposed medical cause for academic failure. As a result, 90% of students classified LD graduate below proficiency, along with 90% of minority and low-income students and 60% of the general population of students.[1] In the best-case scenario, these kids face a lifetime of mediocrity. In the worst-case scenario, these kids experience a tragically poor quality of life.

Imagine if the medical establishment consistently failed to effectively treat 60% to 90% of sick kids. Would we tolerate such failures if we discovered that effective treatments existed but just weren't being used because they conflicted with the beliefs of the medical establishment? We have historically drawn a line in the sand regarding where our beliefs end and science is allowed to take over; medicine is on the science side of that line. We need to draw that same line with respect to education. Our children deserve a science-based education just as they deserve science-based medicine. Their lives depend on *both*.

THE RELIGIOUS ESTABLISHMENT

We have a love/hate relationship with science in this culture. We see scientific discoveries as extremely important in certain areas of human life like medicine, engineering, or agriculture, but most find the applications of science to the understanding of life itself to be quite threatening. Our distrust of science, particularly with respect to matters regarding our existence, our behavior, or the behavior of our children has a long history that warrants discussion as we take on the task of confronting all these establishments I have been talking about.[36] So let's look at religion, the very first establishment, which has had a significant impact on the development of all the others.

The Rise of Anti-Intellectualism

It will come as no surprise to anyone that our country was founded on dissent and a revolt against religious persecution by the aristocracy, which was composed of the intellectual elite.[36] Thus the beginnings of anti-intellectualism were a result of the early colonists' suspicion and distrust of intellectuals, which was understandable in light of the conditions in England they were fleeing. The Founding Fathers were learned men, members of the educated elite, who wrote the Constitution based upon their knowledge of great works in philosophy, law, and politics. However, as the young nation evolved, a great divide began to form between the educated class and the working class — the educated class being those with the wealth and privilege required to afford private tutors and, eventually, private institutions of higher learning. The first such institutions were founded by the educated clergy — those men who pursued religious inquiry from an intellectual perspective.

Working people, particularly rural families, grew increasingly isolated from the areas of the country where education and intellectual pursuits were gaining strength.[36] With this isolation and historic distrust of intellectuals came the emergence of evangelicals, typically working men who felt inspired to speak the word of God to members of their communities. Evangelical preachers rejected the notion that clergy should be educated men. They also rejected the formal, solemn nature of church services typical of the intellectual clergy and encouraged a more passionate, rapturous experience. All of this came to a head during the Great Awakening of the 18th century, the most significant religious revival in our nation's history. Evangelical preachers were against education and "book learning," suggesting that those pursuits interfered with one's ability to truly know God. From this fundamentalist perspective, the only necessary book was the Bible. In contrast, the intellectual clergy largely embraced scientific discoveries and contributions from the scholarly disciplines along with their spiritual pursuits.

Over time, certain areas of the country, starting with New England, continued to hold education in high regard and invested effort in the establishment of schools for the growing population. Organized schools of this sort were slower to be established in the Southern states, where evangelical religion was more common. It was not until the era of Reconstruction following the Civil War that public schools were consistently established in the South.[82]

These early divisions around religion, education, science, and general intellectual pursuits have remained a persistent theme in our country.[24, 36, 64] The anti-intellectualism that is so prevalent today finds its historical origins in the opposing views of the evangelical working class and the intellectual elite. These divides became further solidified with the increasing respect for science that occurred as a result of the influence of Charles Darwin and his theory of evolution, which was perceived as a grave threat by religious fundamentalists. By 1890, Darwin made science increasingly popular in this country and called into question the traditional religious teachings that had previously dominated all aspects of American life — including education.

Our Addiction to Magic and Mysticism

To this day, America is the only Westernized country in the world where evolution remains a controversial subject and is seen as a matter of belief rather than scientific fact.[24, 64] Two-thirds of Americans want creationism to be taught alongside evolution in schools.[24] America also remains the only Westernized country where climate change remains controversial, despite the 99% of climate scientists who have unequivocally confirmed the role of greenhouse gas emissions.[64] Belief in magic and mysticism also remain prominent, with one-third of Americans believing in astrology and four out of five believing in miracles.[24] From this perspective, one can begin to understand the resistance to incorporating scientific practices in our schools and, ultimately, the inability to distinguish between actual scientific evidence and pseudoscience presented as scientific fact. Many Americans have a general distrust of science and a disregard of scientific facts. There is a general view that beliefs should be treated as equal to scientific evidence. Some form of ideology therefore remains the dominant worldview of a large number of Americans, who defend their belief systems despite evidence that such beliefs are erroneous or even harmful. Although science has won the day in many areas of our culture, it remains notably absent in education.

We are addicted to magic and mysticism—the belief in the meta-physical nature of our existence. These beliefs dominate our culture, and we are more likely to accept and encourage those establishments that reflect these beliefs. We want to believe what the educational establishment declares regarding what children should learn and how they should learn it. What the educational establishment believes is also what *we* fundamentally believe. They adopted these beliefs because American culture demanded they do so. We want to believe what the psychological establishment declares regarding the underlying, metaphysical causes of our behavior. We justify these beliefs by aligning them with the medical model, which is based in science and has been scientifically validated. If we can align our beliefs in some way with those that are scientific, then those beliefs must ultimately be true, right? All of these establishments exist and thrive because they justify what we all really think.

The only problem is that often our beliefs result in things fundamentally *not working*. Belief benefits us until, eventually, it doesn't. Then what do we do? What do we do when our beliefs do not work in vastly important areas of human life? What do we do when our beliefs threaten our nation's youth, our economy, our ability to compete globally, or our very existence as a species on this planet? What then? What will it ultimately take for us to give up our beliefs in favor of effective actions? I'm hoping that more than 80 years of failed educational outcomes might be the catalyst to persuade us to take a look at our entrenched beliefs and lead us to ask ourselves, are they worth it?

3

THE OUTCASTS

*"The pragmatic method is primarily a
method of settling metaphysical disputes
that otherwise might be interminable."*
—WILLIAM JAMES[46]

Remember the story about Alex from the introduction? Well, it actually has a happy ending. Not long after that moment with his mom in the parking lot, she pulled Alex out of school altogether and enrolled him full time at Fit Learning for six months. During that period, Alex made over two years' worth of growth in reading, spelling, math, and writing. We also taught him to play chess, and he ended up winning a regional chess tournament. Alex left school performing below grade level and well below the 10th percentile on standard measures of academic achievement. Six months later when he returned to school, he had advanced over two grade levels and was scoring in the highest percentiles on academic achievement measures.

Today, Alex is an accomplished high school student, no longer classified as dyslexic or LD. He has never missed an honor roll, is involved in many extracurricular activities, is a competitive athlete, and has lots of friends. I'm not sure if he still plays chess, though—I need to ask him about that.

The astonishing outcomes we produced with Alex are not an anomaly. These are the kinds of outcomes we produce with our learners every day. Moreover, these are the kinds of outcomes historically produced by behavioral science and the Technology of Teaching. Yet we are the *outcasts*. We aren't members of the establishments. We are the outsiders—excluded from mainstream education and psychology.

As I mentioned earlier, Alex's school team *believed* he was disabled. They attributed his academic struggles to a learning disability. From their perspective, the most that could be hoped for was to help Alex learn to live with his disability or *accommodate* his disability in some way. Remember, the school recommended he stop trying to read altogether and that his mother give him audio recordings of books instead. The cause of Alex's reading deficits was believed to reside inside of him—rooted in faulty wiring or dysfunctional neurology.

I saw Alex very differently. I saw Alex as a kid who hadn't mastered basic skills, not because of a disability but because he had never been provided with the opportunity to master them. I also saw Alex as a kid who had learned some really bad habits, which interfered with his learning and mastering effective skills. As I mentioned before, Alex had been specifically taught to guess words. Unfortunately, schools teach many kids to read this way. Some kids are lucky enough to have learned phonics and word attack skills somewhere along the way too, so this word-guessing habit might not prove as detrimental because they have another strategy to use when they guess a word incorrectly. But Alex hadn't learned phonics and word attack skills, so his only option was the word-guessing habit he had been taught, which eventually resulted in his being diagnosed with dyslexia. Can you imagine doing exactly as your teachers tell you and then being told you are disabled because of it? What a dehumanizing experience for a kid.

I didn't attribute Alex's skills deficits to there being something wrong with him. I attributed his skills deficits to there being something wrong with his learning history. So I changed that learning history by providing him with effective instruction and repeated, reinforced practice of skills to mastery. As a result, in six short months, Alex became an accomplished reader and student. His mastery of skills was my responsibility, *not his*. It was my job to design the learning environment in such a way that he mastered skills. And because of behavioral science and the Technology of Teaching, I was able to do that. Alex was never disabled. Alex's school environment was disabled.

Now you are going to meet the outcasts—the behavioral scientists and their corresponding discoveries about learning, which lead to the design of profoundly effective teaching practices. I am also going to attempt to illustrate why this science proves so difficult for many people to accept—particularly members of the establishments.

THE NATURAL SCIENCE OF BEHAVIOR

During that shift in the zeitgeist in America at the turn of the 20th century that I described in Chapter 2, another developing branch of psychology asserted that the study of human behavior should move forward as a natural science.[45] It was argued that psychology should focus on observable *behavior* as its subject matter because it was objective and measurable. This group of scientists focused on the behavior of the whole organism in relation to its historical and current context. From this perspective, a scientific understanding of the interaction between the entire behaving person and their environment would lead to the prediction and influence of human behavior, and thus the potential to improve the quality of human life.[83–85] Although the view of behavior as the appropriate subject matter for psychology might seem fairly innocuous, such a perspective has been a historic source of controversy for the establishments. To better understand the establishments' reluctance to accept behavioral science, we must consider the historical context through which this science has evolved.

E. L. Thorndike's work at the turn of the 20th century marked the beginning of the scientific study of learning in America.[86, 87] His empirical work led to the discovery of the law of effect, one of the first scientific principles to emerge regarding the role of consequences in determining behavior. Unfortunately, due to the nature of his experimental methods, he was unable to make the monumental discoveries regarding learning and behavior that eventually led to the development of radical behaviorism and the natural science of behavior, which has given rise to the Technology of Teaching that I will describe later. These discoveries were not made until much later, when B. F. Skinner began his early work in operant conditioning during the 1930s.[83] The means of bringing the science of learning into the design of teaching practices did not yet exist at the turn of the century during that crucial period of educational reform.

Moreover, the philosophy of radical behaviorism and the view that human behavior could be studied through natural science did not, and does not, fit with the ideology of our culture. The notion that behavior might largely be environmentally determined was, and remains, blasphemous to many people. What about the soul? What about personality? What about the characteristics that make us uniquely human? You can't leave these out! From this perspective, leaving these out reduces us to automatons and relegates us to the level of other animals who don't possess a mind or a soul. And therein lies the rub.

What I am offering is that a natural science of behavior provides the solution to many human crises — education being one among many others. This science has led to remarkable discoveries regarding how we learn everything from the most basic skills to the most complex forms of cognition. It has led to the prediction and influence of human behavior in ways that vastly improve quality of life. Most people are unaware that this science exists because, as I have said, it is not part of the establishments that we have previously met. The natural science of behavior has been ostracized, boycotted, excluded, marginalized, ignored, and ultimately relegated to small corners in the greater culture. But quietly, elegantly, and pragmatically, we have been developing a science that potentially holds the key to saving us all.

Now, accepting this science and its corresponding discoveries means going into a bit of a detox. It means giving up our addictions to metaphysical causes and the practice of naming things as a means of explaining them. Accepting this science means getting a little uncomfortable. But if you stick with me, you might see how behavioral science is actually not so scary. You might see that behavioral scientists are true humanitarians who hold the same values as you do. We value a high quality of life for all humans. We believe that all children can be educated effectively and have the fundamental right to that kind of education. We value using this science to help others live a life of happiness, protect their loved ones, access valuable resources, and ensure their own survival. We view behavioral science as a means of ensuring the survival of the human race.

Hypothetical Constructs and Explanatory Fictions

The natural science of behavior is fundamentally about learning. From our perspective, learning is best defined as *the change in behavior over time*.[88] Although the educational establishment wants to appeal to more obtuse, subjective definitions of learning, such definitions have led us down an aimless path with a majority of children failing to be properly educated.

Traditional notions of learning tend to refer to inaccessible constructs such as the acquisition of knowledge, understanding, intelligence, or awareness; however, I challenge any educator to directly measure learning defined in this way. Regardless of how learning is defined, the only option is to measure performance or a learner's *behavior* with respect to a subject matter. Traditionally, after a learner's performance is measured, inferences are made regarding what that performance means with respect to what the establishments regard as the true objectives of education, such as gaining knowledge, understanding, insight, or intellect. However, such inferences are not *real*. They are hypothetical constructs imposed upon the behavior of the learner that actually interfere with where the focus should be — the learner's behavior.

Hypothetical constructs are notorious sources of trouble, yet they dominate the establishments. As we've seen, learning disability labels are classic examples of the trouble that arises when trying to explain something via a construct. For example, learners like Alex who struggle with reading are often given a diagnosis of dyslexia. Dyslexia is a term that describes a set of behaviors often engaged in by poor readers such as word-guessing, phoneme insertions or substitutions, word skipping, and word or letter reversals. Each of the previously described are *behaviors* that the learner engages in when presented with reading material. In other words, these are things learners *do*.

From problematic things that some learners do when reading, an inference is made about why they do these things. Giving a learner a diagnosis of dyslexia is seen as an explanation for the problematic reading repertoire. However, the only way a learner is diagnosed is based upon their performance (i.e., behavior) on a set of assessments where inferences are then made about this performance, and more often than not, an inferred neurological dysfunction (i.e., dyslexia) is said to account for the reading problem. To be clear, there is no direct evidence of a neurological dysfunction. The only information available is that of the learner's performance—behavior—on a set of assessments. Everything else is inferred.

Once such a diagnosis is given as an explanation of a reading problem, a vicious cycle of circular reasoning begins with little hope for effective action. *Why is Alex such a poor reader? Because he has dyslexia. How do you know he has dyslexia? Because he is such a poor reader.* Around and around we go. Dyslexia is an explanatory fiction. A label has been used to describe a deficient behavioral repertoire, which still requires explanation if it is ever to be changed or improved.

The medicalization of skills deficits has tragic implications. In the traditional view, children *have* learning disabilities. The verb alone communicates volumes about how such learners are perceived. Due to inferences made regarding the behavior of learners, learning disability labels resemble the disease model in medicine. Just as one might *have* strep throat or the flu, learners are said to *have* a learning disability. But no blood test or medical procedure exists that provides direct evidence that deficient behavioral repertoires have a physiological cause. The only evidence of a learning disability stems from behavioral measures.

In this sense, learning disabilities are a *doing* not a *having*. Learners *do* things that become classified as evidence of some disability. Sadly, once learners have been classified as LD, educators are absolved of responsibility for effectively educating them. As in Alex's case, failure to learn is erroneously attributed to the hypothetical disability so that ineffective teaching practices remain unexamined and unchanged.

Learning disability labels are not the only explanatory fictions that interfere with the design of more effective teaching practices. Explaining a student's poor academic performance as caused by inherent laziness or a lack of intelligence is just as problematic. As for IQ, it is also viewed as something people *have*; however, the only evidence for IQ stems from performance on IQ tests. Specific types of behaviors are measured by IQ tests and then hypothetical inferences are made based upon these behaviors. To put it bluntly, IQ is not *real*. It cannot be directly measured or observed. It is a hypothetical construct used to explain patterns of behavior.

Work ethic, self-determination, self-confidence, self-esteem, and other labels are also often attributed to individuals based on their observed behavior. All of these things result in explanations being seen as inherent to the individual rather than as a result of a history of specific interactions between a learner and their environment, which have given rise to their behaving in such a way. The more inherent the explanation, the less accessible it is, and thus, the less we can understand it.

The current notions regarding learning disabilities, IQ, or personality characteristics as *causes* for learning, or the failure to learn, resemble similarly prescientific explanations that previously dominated the field of medicine. For example, before the dawn of modern science, imbalanced humors were hypothesized to be the cause of all human ailments. Black bile, yellow bile, phlegm, and blood were hypothesized to be the four common elements, or humors, of the human body similar to the elements of the earth. Though these substances clearly exist within the human body, it was the inferences about their causal role in all things that was a problem. Black bile was associated with melancholy, the earth, winter, old age, Saturn, cold and dry climates, and the spleen. Phlegm was associated with water, autumn, maturity, cold and moist climates, the brain, and the moon. Causal agency was given to the humors' associations and provided as explanations for ailments. Such notions seem ludicrous in light of advancements in science and modern medicine. However, at the time, these theories were believed to be true and techniques developed to balance the humors, though frequently leading to death, were adopted and practiced by physicians.

At the time, the success of such practices mattered less than the fact that the practices matched what people *believed* to be the causes of sickness. Belief as the ultimate evaluative criteria, regardless of evidence to the contrary, defines ideology and prescientific practices. Ideology dominates our culture and has given rise to the establishments. It is most recognizable in organized religion where belief or faith is the guiding force. However, ideology also runs the show in education and psychology, though it is frequently, and dangerously, masked as science. The fact that ineffective educational traditions have persisted for close to a century demonstrates the dangers of ideology in an institution that should favor pragmatic values. In other words, education should be about what works.

If the purpose of our educational system is to educate the majority of American children, then pragmatism should serve as our guiding value. Ensuring that teachers do what works should be the *only* evaluative criteria. However, as I previously articulated, ideology runs the show in education, where teaching practices are evaluated in terms of whether they reflect the beliefs of the educational establishment regardless of whether or not these practices are effective.

Behavior Is Primary

Behavioral science rejects explanatory fictions and hypothetical constructs in favor of the analysis of observable behavior in relation to specific features of a person's environment.

Behavioral science is a *natural science,* along with scientific disciplines such as biology, chemistry, and physics.

These sciences are not ideological, prescientific, or pseudoscientific. These sciences do not explain phenomena with hypothetical constructs. These sciences discover causal relationships in the world and do not confuse correlations with causations. These sciences explain natural phenomena through direct observation, measurement, and the systematic manipulation of variables over time until laws or principles are discovered and described. Descriptions of laws or principles of natural phenomena are not the same as hypothetical constructs. Constructs are *inferences* about what was actually observed. Laws or principles are descriptions of a consistent pattern of observed events in relation to identified variables. Descriptions of causal relations and hypothetical constructs created to explain events are two very different things.

Contrary to popular belief, behavioral science also acknowledges those aspects of human beings that are not observable by others and, thus, appear more metaphysical in nature, such as thinking, imagining, remembering, and the like.[84, 89, 90] However, from the perspective of our science, these activities are not metaphysical at all. They are *behavioral*. In other words, these are also things humans *do* and, more important, humans *learn to do them* in the same manner as they learn everything else. The only difference is that these behaviors are private or occur inside the skin, and thus, are not observable by others. In this way, these behaviors cannot be the subject matter of natural science unless we somehow make them public or observable. Later we'll see how private behavior, like thinking, can actually be made public, and so become amenable to understanding through natural science.

Significant discoveries that have led to the survival and advancement of the human species can be traced to the natural sciences. However, as I have previously stated, these kinds of advances have never been made with respect to educational practices. But who will make the essential discoveries that further our species' advancement and ensure its survival if the majority of our citizens fail to be properly educated? The time for a natural science of education is now. Moreover, as I will show, a natural science of education already exists where significant discoveries have been made regarding the nature of learning; however, this science has been at best ignored and, at worst, intentionally blocked by the establishments.

THE PRINCIPLES OF LEARNING

Let us turn to the laws or principles of learning that have been discovered in behavioral science. Again, the discoveries I am going to share with you have been made based on measuring observable behavior over time in relation to the systematic manipulation of variables in the environment. In this sense, behavioral science adheres to the basic tenets of any natural science. It is *inductive* in that the phenomenon (i.e., behavior) is directly observed and measured over time. It focuses on the behavior of the *individual* rather than the group where specific instances of a phenomenon are evaluated repeatedly over time such that generalities are eventually made. It employs the *scientific method* in that variables in the environment are systematically manipulated and the effects of this manipulation evaluated with respect to the behavior during its ongoing observation and measurement. It *systematically replicates* the manipulation of variables over time, which leads to the discovery of generalities: laws or principles of behavior.

I realize that I have used the term *manipulation* a lot at this point, which may come across as a bit scary. What I mean by manipulation is simply that we adjust some feature of the environment and then measure the effects that this adjustment has on whatever behavior we are trying to change. We aren't manipulating people in some sinister way. I will illustrate this point further in the next section.

The summary of discoveries I am about to provide is in no way exhaustive. A comprehensive overview of the vast discoveries made in behavioral science is beyond the scope of this book. I refer you to the references provided if you wish to explore this topic further. [83–85, 88–97]

Behavior Is Selected by its Consequences

Through the process of natural science, it has been discovered that behavior is *selected* by its consequences.[91, 93] In other words, behavior is strengthened or weakened by that which *follows* it. A consequence is called "reinforcing," or "a reinforcer," if it strengthens the behavior it follows or makes it *more likely* to happen again. A consequence is called "punishing," or a "punisher," if it weakens the behavior it follows or makes it *less likely* it will happen again. We have evolved as a species to learn through this process, and it is the natural science of behavior that led to the discovery of this fundamental principle. This principle is not based on opinion or ideology. It stems from discoveries made through natural science. It is a scientific fact that has been erroneously ignored and worse, rejected by the establishments since its discovery. However, the attempts to refute this principle stem from ideology, not empirical evidence.

The notion of selection by consequences is a difficult one for the establishments to accept. The idea that behavior is ultimately caused by something that *follows* it is pretty counterintuitive, right? When we think of cause-effect relations, we typically think of the cause coming *before* the effect. For example, if we push a boulder down a hill, it rolled down the hill because we pushed it. In other words, we pushed it first and then it rolled down the hill. Well, I am about to blow your minds, but this same cause-effect analysis goes out the window for behavior. Behavioral science has led to the discovery that the reverse is actually true.

Imagine an infant lying in their crib with a mobile hanging within their reach. Because of how we have evolved, infants are in a constant state of motion when awake—frequently moving their arms, legs, head, eyes, and mouth. In other words, infants are constantly *behaving*. Behavior of this sort is reflexive at first. So, imagine an infant lying in their crib, reflexively moving their arms and legs about. Suddenly, one of their arms accidentally makes contact with the mobile hanging over their crib and, as a result, the mobile moves. Movement in the visual field is powerfully reinforcing for most infants. So that random arm motion has just been reinforced, or selected, by the movement of the mobile.

It is now more likely that the infant is going to move their arm that way again and, if they do and it is again followed by the reinforcing movement of the mobile, this behavior will become stronger (i.e., more likely to continue to occur). Over time, that specific arm motion will occur more frequently to the point where it will appear as if the infant is "intentionally" moving their arm to make the mobile move. What has actually happened, however, is that the infant's arm motion has been *selected* through repeated reinforcement of that behavior over time, and thus, that behavior has been *learned*. That arm motion is no longer reflexive or random; it is now a learned behavior and it was learned through its repeated reinforcement over time.

In the above example, the "cause" of the infant moving their arm so that the mobile moves can be traced to what happened *after* they moved their arm that way in the past. I promise you the infant didn't say to themselves ahead of time, "I think I will try to make that mobile move," and subsequently work to accomplish that goal. The event was initially an accident. The infant was just randomly moving their arms and legs about. But, in an instant, one of those behaviors accidentally came into contact with a reinforcing consequence in the environment and, boom, the conditions for learning occurred. Now, if that infant had never been placed back in that crib again or had never accidentally moved the mobile more than once, it is unlikely that anything would have been learned. But if that infant was placed back in that crib time and time again, and their arm motion successfully moved that mobile enough, then learning would occur. And that's how it works. The beauty of the learning process astounds me.

This same learning process occurs for all humans and all behaviors. Infants, toddlers, young children, teenagers, and adults all learn via the consequences of their behavior. Of course, the kinds of behaviors being learned become vastly more complex than an arm motion that makes a mobile move, but the process is the same regardless. Unfortunately, when not understood, this process serves as a frequent source of frustration for parents.

For example, infants cry a lot, and this behavior is frequently followed by reinforcement such as being fed, being held, having their diaper changed, or being stimulated in some way. Again, crying is initially reflexive illustrated by the fact that infants cry immediately upon leaving the womb. We have evolved in this way as crying contributes to an infant's survival. However, over time, crying actually becomes learned in the same manner as described for the arm motion that moved the mobile.

As infants become toddlers, they must learn to access reinforcement in more appropriate ways, like through the learning of words and phrases. Remember, kids have a long history of reinforcement for crying, so this is a well-established behavior in toddlers. Suddenly, crying doesn't work as well anymore because toddlers are expected to do something else instead. This transition period can be rough. Remember my reference to the "terrible twos" and how this developmental stage is often used to explain the notorious tantrums of toddlers? Well, the "terrible twos" is real, but not because of some developmental stage. The tantrums of toddlers are explained by a long history of reinforcement for crying throughout infancy.

Let's imagine we have a toddler who, like all children, has a long history of reinforcement for crying but is now learning some words and simple phrases, like "mommy," "daddy," "cookie," and "juice, please." Picture a scenario where this toddler is thirsty, and her cup of juice is on the counter above her reach. Let's also pretend mom is talking on the phone. Our toddler might initially attempt to reach the juice herself. If this attempt proves unsuccessful, she might toddle over to mom, pull on her pants leg, and say "juice." If mom happens to notice, she might reach over, grab the juice cup, and hand it to her toddler. At this moment, mom has just created a powerful learning opportunity for her child. She has just reinforced her toddler saying "juice," and has increased the likelihood that her toddler will behave this way again.

However, this scenario could go another way. Mom might not notice her toddler's behavior at first, as she is deep in conversation on the phone. So what might her toddler do at this point? She might pull harder on mom's leg and say "juice" again. If mom still doesn't notice these communicative behaviors, what do you think might happen? It's highly likely that our toddler is going to start whining, crying, or throwing a full-blown tantrum. As I have said, these behaviors have a long history of reinforcement, so they have a high probability of occurrence. It's also highly likely that when our toddler starts behaving in this more unpleasant way, mom is certainly going to notice, and unfortunately, mom is probably going to hand her toddler the juice. Mom has created a powerful learning opportunity for her child at this moment too. Unfortunately, in this version of the scenario, mom reinforced crying rather than saying "juice."

In the first scenario, our toddler's verbal skills were reinforced, increasing the probability that she will use this word again. In the second scenario, our toddler's crying was reinforced, and more important, her saying "juice" was ignored. So our toddler in the second scenario is more likely to cry again and less likely to say "juice." Think of the hundreds of thousands of moments like these kids have throughout the course of their development. It is literally dumb luck that kids learn to speak at all because crying is such an established behavior from birth.

Some parents understand the power of consequences from a commonsense perspective, and intentionally reinforce appropriate behavior and ignore or redirect inappropriate behavior as much as possible. However, many parents don't understand this principle and actually receive advice from so-called parenting experts that results in their reinforcing a lot of inappropriate behaviors. Unfortunately, many kids raised in this way aren't much fun to be around and some even eventually receive diagnoses of various sorts, like speech language delay, attention deficit disorder, oppositional defiance disorder, and the like. As I've explained, these diagnoses simply *name* a pattern of behavior, they don't explain it. The explanation for these behaviors can be found in the child's history of reinforcement for behaving in undesirable ways and the lack of reinforcement for behaving in more appropriate ways.

The establishments also have a hard time with the principle of selection by consequences because this principle really deals in future probabilities, which are counterintuitive compared with their immediate effects. Let's go back to the scenario of the toddler throwing a tantrum while her mom is on the phone. Do you think the toddler continued to tantrum after she was given the juice? Not likely. The toddler most likely stopped crying the moment her mom gave her the juice. So problem solved, right? And therein lies the source of confusion for most.

In the immediate moment, it seems like mom solved the problem. Her daughter started crying, she gave her daughter what she wanted, and the crying stopped. Unfortunately, the problem has only been made worse, but the effects of that worsening aren't immediately detectable. In the moment, things got better. It is only by considering this pattern of behavior *over time* that the long-term effects become apparent. Her child may have stopped crying in the moment, but the next time her child wants something that she can't access, it is highly likely she is going to cry. Moreover, she will likely start crying more frequently, more intensely, and for longer durations of time. The learning process doesn't happen in an instant. The learning process occurs over time, and the effects must be evaluated from this perspective.

So, the principle of selection by consequences often requires that we act counterintuitively. When our toddler is throwing a fit, our immediate tendency is to do whatever it takes to get them to stop. This tendency is simply the result of our own learning history. A toddler throwing a tantrum is unpleasant, and we will work to escape or avoid such unpleasant moments. In other words, we will do anything it takes to get the toddler to calm down or prevent the toddler from becoming upset in the first place.

Effective parenting requires us to ignore our natural urge to escape an unpleasant situation. In moments like these, we have to do the exact opposite of what we want to do. What we should actually do is ignore the child completely until they have calmed down. Once calm, we should prompt them to say or do something more appropriate before we give them what they want that occasioned the tantrum in the first place. However, this kind of parenting is not easy. It requires lots and lots of practice.

This kind of parenting is also made more difficult by the widely held cultural belief that young children should never be upset. When young children throw tantrums in public, most believe such tantrums are reflective of bad parenting. Only bad parents have badly behaved children. Good parents have children who never misbehave. Such cultural beliefs lead to the perpetuation of parenting practices that actually produce long-term behavior problems in children. We should actually smile and clap for parents who bravely ignore their children's tantrums in public. We should pat them on the back and ask if they need help or support. Unfortunately, what typically happens is that people frown, shake their heads, or roll their eyes. In other words, parents of misbehaving children receive frequent and intense public shaming. To avoid this shaming, parents do whatever it takes to avoid their children's upset, and more often than not, end up reinforcing inappropriate behavior and ensuring that the problem continues or gets worse.

Upset is an essential part of the learning process. When an undesirable behavior has a long history of reinforcement, it is going to get worse before it gets better. It takes time to get rid of old habits and replace them with new ones. Learning doesn't happen overnight. It takes lots and lots of reinforced practice.

As a culture, we like immediate gratification. We want to snap our fingers and have things magically change. Unfortunately, learning doesn't work this way. Learning occurs in time and takes time to occur. So parenting requires a long-term perspective. Rather than immediately reacting in the moment to stop a child from being upset, we must pause and consider the consequences of what we are about to do. Do I want to get my child to stop crying now or do I want to help my child learn more appropriate ways to communicate that will contribute to her development over time? The discoveries of behavioral science suggest that parents should pause and consider the long-term effects of their reactions, even if it means that the immediate moment may continue to be unpleasant and there may be some public embarrassment.

Stimuli in the Environment Gain Meaning Through Consequences

Behavioral science has also led to discoveries about how stimuli—or features of the environment—gain meaning or acquire *functions*.[59, 90, 91] The function of a stimulus refers to its effects on behavior or what a person *does* in its presence. Let's consider a cup, for example, which is a *stimulus* or a feature of the environment. A cup does not magically produce the word "cup" from a toddler because this word is suddenly known due to inborn forces inside the brain. Rather, the presence of a cup can lead a toddler to say the word "cup" through a history of reinforcement for seeing a cup, being prompted to say "cup," saying the word "cup," and having the saying of the word followed by reinforcement of some sort, such as being given the cup or being provided with praise after the word is spoken.

Moreover, stimuli that share common features with those that have been previously associated with reinforcement can also come to have meaning, or functions, without having to be directly learned. In other words, the functions of stimuli generalize to other stimuli such that novel features of a child's environment can also come to evoke meaningful responding without direct training.[59] For example, a child who learns to name one specific cup will begin spontaneously naming other unknown objects as cups if they share similar features with the original cup. This type of generalization accounts for the explosion in learning that occurs in early childhood.

Children have hundreds of thousands of these types of learning experiences through the natural course of their development. The learning process that is occurring is undetectable for most lay people. It may appear as if toddlers are starting to name things and display other new skills simply as part of their physical development. However, age is not the controlling factor in learning. Though not widely understood, the critical factors in young children's acquisition of new skills and features of their environments coming to have meaning, *or functions,* result from specific ways they behave in response to stimuli and, most important, repeated reinforcement of those behaviors over time.

Language Is Behavior: It Is Learned and Selected by Consequences

Many critics of behavioral science suggest that the learning process described above cannot possibly account for the acquisition of complex forms of human behavior. Learning an arm motion or to name an object is one thing, but human language is vastly more complex, right? How does this simple process account for thinking, problem-solving, remembering, or imagining? But our science has discovered that complex language repertoires evolve from the very same process as that involved in the infant learning to move their arm in a specific way or a toddler learning to name objects in the environment.[90, 98–100] Language involves responding relationally, or responding to one event in terms of another, and we learn to respond this way through a history of reinforcement.

Let's return to our example of a toddler learning to name a cup. In that example, a toddler was shown a cup and learned to say "cup" when presented with it. However, throughout the course of a child's development, other types of responses will also be reinforced. For example, a parent may say "Where's the cup?" or "Give me the cup," and provide prompting and reinforcement when the child finds the cup, points to the cup, or gives the parent the cup. Again, children have hundreds of thousands of these kinds of learning experiences.

Over time, the child acquires a generalized ability to respond *bidirectionally*. By bidirectionally, I simply mean being able to *see a thing—say its name* and *hear the name of a thing—and find the thing*. For example, a child may initially learn through direct training to name an item when presented with it, such as see a picture of an octopus and learn to say "octopus." But as a result of their general-ized ability to respond *bidirectionally*, this same child, who has only directly learned to name an octopus from its picture, will also be able to find the picture of an octopus among many other pictures on the *first* occasion of being asked "Where's the octopus" or "Can you find the octopus?" Moreover, this same child, who only directly learned to name an octopus from its picture, will also be able to spontaneously respond to questions like "Which ones are not the octopus?" or "Show me all of the animals other than the octopus." And because of the generative nature of bidirectional responding, the reverse is also true. In other words, a child could be directly trained to point only to the octopus among an array of pictures when instructed to "Find the octo-pus,"and as a result of that training the child can then spontaneously say "octopus" when presented with a picture of it, even though this naming response was never directly trained. The naming response was *derived* as a result of learning to point to a picture of an octopus upon hearing "Where's the octopus?" or "Find the octopus."

Bidirectional responding of this sort is a generalized skill learned over time through a history of reinforcement for responding in this manner. Over time, a child need only receive reinforcement for respond-ing to a new feature of the environment in one way and will then spon-taneously derive responding to that feature in many other ways. Thus, simply naming objects quickly becomes conceptual in nature.

As the learning process progresses, responding moves from the concrete to the abstract, where children can begin to frame relations among stimuli in increasingly arbitrary ways. Through a history of reinforcement, children can begin to respond *relationally* in terms of similarity, difference, comparison, opposition, hierarchy, and so forth.[90, 98–100]

To clarify what I mean by responding relationally, rather than simply saying "cup" in the presence of a cup, children learn to respond to objects in terms of relational categories like sameness, difference, relative size or value, or class membership. For example, they learn to identify if one cup is the *same as* or *different from* another cup. They learn to identify one cup as *larger* or *smaller* than another. They learn to classify cups into categories like *things in the kitchen, things I drink out of, things that I can put stuff into*, or *household items*.

This type of relational responding always begins with an object's physical attributes. Children first learn to identify objects that are *physically* larger, smaller, more, or less in relation to other objects. As this repertoire is established, children begin to respond in this same way to *arbitrary* relations among stimuli or in ways not determined by the physical attributes of a thing. For example, a nickel may be physically larger than a dime, but a dime has greater value than a nickel. So the attribute of more or less has nothing to do with the physical difference in size between a nickel and dime. The value of the coin is completely arbitrary, created only verbally. In this way, relations such as more or less come to be arbitrarily applied and children learn to apply them through a history of reinforcement.[99]

As bidirectional responding is established and children begin to derive relations in arbitrary ways, they begin deriving more complex relations.[90, 98] For example, we have already seen how a child can come to spontaneously respond to stimuli in a bidirectional manner, such as to learn to name an octopus from a picture of an octopus and then, without training, find an octopus among many sea creatures. However, children also come to derive other types of complex relations.

For example, imagine a child is told that Tommy is taller than Sally and Sally is taller than Jimmy. From those verbal relations, a child can derive that Sally is shorter than Tommy and Jimmy is shorter than

Sally. However, the child can also derive that Jimmy is shorter than Tommy — even though Tommy and Jimmy were never presented in relation to one another. This child has never met Tommy, Sally, or Jimmy and has no familiarity with their physical size. The child is informed of their relative size only through language; that is, verbally. Again, this type of complex relational responding is not magical, although it certainly can appear that way to the layperson. Rather, it develops as a function of a history of reinforcement for responding in this manner such that it becomes established as a generative skill or ability.[90, 98]

As children begin acquiring more complex language skills in the manner described above, their ability to respond relationally can actually transform the functions, or *meanings*, of other stimuli in their environment.[90, 98] For example, imagine that a child is at a video arcade and is told that black tokens awarded for winning a game are worth more than gold ones when exchanged for prizes. This arbitrary relation can transform the function or meaning of games that award black tokens *before* the child actually plays them.

By simply being told about the arbitrary value of black versus gold tokens, the games that award black tokens become more reinforcing. Thus, these games will now evoke a greater motivation to play them, even if the games that award black tokens are fundamentally more difficult to play or require longer wait times to access them. Children will work harder to play the games awarding black tokens simply as a function of the greater arbitrary value granted to them. The function or meaning of the game has been transformed for that child before the child has even played it, won any black tokens, or exchanged black tokens for prizes. These kinds of complex networks of relations in the world actually define language and, ultimately, what it means to be human.[90, 98]

Complex Repertoires Are Gradually Shaped Over Time

The above discussion of the gradual acquisition of complex language repertoires over time through a history of reinforcement leads us to *shaping:* another fundamental principle of learning.[2, 59–63, 83, 91, 101] Shaping entails the gradual progression of skills from smaller components to more complex repertoires. We have evolved as a species to learn this way, and it often happens naturally in the environment as a result of accidental reinforcement or commonsense teaching practices.

For example, through repeated reinforcement, a child may first make some sort of approximation to the word "cup" in the presence of an actual cup, such as "cu" or "up." But as a child can more reliably produce that approximation, a caregiver might prompt the child to say the entire word "cup" before providing reinforcement. Again, there are hundreds of thousands of examples of this process occurring throughout the course of a child's development.

We would never expect a child to begin speaking in sentences. Children begin making small utterances that are gradually *shaped* into simple words and finally full sentences through the reinforcement of successive approximations. When truly understood as a scientific process, shaping results in the intentional design of profoundly effective teaching practices.

On the other hand, a lack of understanding of the shaping process has tragic implications for teaching practices. Consider Alex, for example. Alex had never effectively mastered the essential component skills for reading: identifying the sounds of letters or applying them to the decoding of unknown words. However, in his school environment, he was expected to read anyway. His teachers tried to teach him some tricks—like word-guessing based on the first letter—but these tricks didn't lead to his being able to effectively read. The result: He was diagnosed with a reading disability. However, as I hope I have made clear, Alex wasn't disabled at all. He was just being expected to perform a complex behavioral repertoire before the components required to perform that repertoire had been practiced and strengthened through reinforcement.

Schools like to skip over basic steps. Schools like to start with complicated skills without a consideration of all of the necessary basic skills required for performing the complex repertoire. Learning doesn't work this way. Learning complex repertoires requires reinforcement of successive approximations of that complex skill through shaping. Sadly, because shaping is not intentionally used for the design of teaching practices, a majority of students fail to acquire mastery of prerequisite skills, and many are then diagnosed with a learning disability as a result.

Behavior Is Measured as Rate. Learning Is Measured as Celeration.

At this point in the book, I hope you now recognize that behavior matters. What we *do* is the primary subject matter of behavioral science. You also now know that behavior is selected by consequences over time. The gradual selection of behavior by consequences over time defines the learning process. We behave in some way, that behavior comes into contact with some consequence in the environment, and that consequence, if it is reinforcing, makes the behavior more likely to occur again. If that consequence is punishing, it will make the behavior less likely to occur again. In this way, consequences are defined in terms of their *future effects* on behavior. But how can we possibly predict the future? How can we know if a behavior is more or less likely to occur again?

We predict the future probability of a behavior through measurement, B. F. Skinner's greatest contribution to the world, though his work has been historically mischaracterized and tragically overlooked by the establishments. Through his research on operant conditioning, Skinner discovered that *rate of response*, which is defined as count per time, is the fundamental measure of behavior. [83, 91] As with all the natural sciences, behavioral science employs measures based on the fundamental properties of the phenomenon of interest (i.e., behavior).

Behavior occurs in time and takes time to occur. Behavior is repeatable and thus countable. Count and time are the fundamental properties of behavior, and thus determine the unit used to measure it.[88]

From this, Skinner derived and subsequently demonstrated that rate of response (also known as frequency of response) is the most sensitive, universal, and absolute measure of behavior.[88] For the remainder of this book, I will use *rate* to refer to our fundamental unit of measurement, though Skinner and other pioneers in our field used rate and frequency interchangeably.[88] To avoid confusion, I am going to stick with the term *rate* moving forward. Just remember that rate is measured as count per time.

Let's go back to our infant in the crib. Let's say we want to measure their arm moving behavior to objectively determine if learning is taking place. To do this, we must first define the behavior in a way that enables us to accurately count it. Let's define the behavior as "moving the arm such that it moves the mobile." So we are counting only those arm movements that result in the mobile moving. We now have our behavioral definition or what we are going to count.

Next, we must count the occurrence of this specific behavior for a set period of time or our measurement won't make any sense. If we use count without time, it becomes difficult to interpret what the count actually means. If I report that a behavior occurred 10 times, can you easily determine if this behavior occurred frequently or infrequently? Was it 10 times per minute, per day, per hour, per month? The time dimension provides essential information about the strength, and therefore probability, of a behavior. We must always count a behavior within some standard unit of time.

Let's pretend that we decide to observe the infant across several one-minute time periods, counting each instance of arm movement as we have defined it during each one-minute period. Let's pretend that the first time we measure, the infant engages in two instances of moving their arm in a way that moves the mobile: a rate of two per minute. The next time we measure, we count five of these movements in a minute: a rate of five per minute. And the next time we measure, we count 10 of these movements in a minute: a rate of 10 per minute. We now have a measure of the change in rate over time.

The rate of the infant's arm-moving behavior increased from two per minute to 10 per minute, so the infant increased their rate of arm-moving by a factor of five across the observations. In other words, they were behaving five times more in the last observation as compared with the first one because an increase from two to ten is a *times five* increase (i.e., 2 x 5 = 10). We can now confidently say that the infant is "learning" to move their arm in such a way that it moves the mobile because their rate has dramatically increased over time. We can predict that the infant will continue moving their arm in this manner, and that the rate will probably continue to increase because their change in rate over time suggests that this is likely to happen.

Now, let's imagine that when we initially measured the infant's behavior, their rate didn't change, or it even decreased. Let's pretend that we counted two per minute, zero per minute, and one per minute across our observations. Would we be able to confidently say that the infant was learning and predict that the behavior was going to continue to occur or get stronger? No, because the rate is actually decreasing. What if we wanted to try to increase the chances that the infant learned this behavior? Can we adjust, or *manipulate*, the environment in some way to make learning more likely? Yes, we can!

Let's say that we notice that the mobile is just out of the infant's normal reach and, in order to make contact with it, the infant must move their arm significantly upward, but they don't make this motion very often. The current position of the mobile makes it less likely that the infant's arm will accidentally make contact with it. What if we brought the mobile closer to make it more likely that a normal arm motion would result in the mobile moving? So we try this intervention. We lower the mobile slightly so that it is well within the infant's reach.

In this way, we *manipulated* the environment by adjusting the height of the mobile. Again, nothing scary or sinister here. We simply adjusted a feature of the environment.

Now we can measure the rate of their behavior again and see if our intervention had any effect. We count the behavior across several one-minute time periods, and we get rates of two per minute, eight per minute, and 12 per minute. Did lowering the mobile increase the rate of their behavior? Yes! Now we have behavior that has increased from two per minute to 12 per minute (i.e., a *times six* increase). We can now confidently say that learning is occurring!

I have asserted that, from the perspective of natural science, learning is best defined as *the change in behavior over time*.[88] In our example with the infant, their rate of arm moving changed over time by increasing or getting faster. Since the rate of their behavior significantly increased over time, we can derive that learning occurred. In behavioral science, learning is quantified by our measure of *celeration*.[88, 102]

Another pioneer in our field, Ogden Lindsley, also made a monumental contribution to the world that is completely overlooked by the establishments. He created a graphic tool called the Standard Celeration Chart, which we call the SCC for short. Using this graph (which Ogden Lindsley preferred to call a chart rather than a graph), rate can be plotted across time (e.g., days, weeks, months, or years) such that standard slopes are produced from lines of best fit drawn through these data points.[102] The slopes produced by these lines of best fit are called *celerations* (akin to the acceleration and deceleration of moving objects), which literally translates into change in rate over time or count per time per time per time. For example, count per minute per day per week gives us a *weekly celeration,* or how much learning occurred in a week. Count per day per week per month gives us a *monthly celeration,* or how much learning occurred in a month.

Let's go back to our infant example and pretend that each time we measured the rate of our infant's arm-moving behavior, we plotted it on the SCC—the standard graphic tool Ogden Lindsley created for us. Below, you will see an SCC I created reflecting the hypothetical data we collected of our infant's arm-moving behavior.[103]

Each black dot on the chart represents the rate we measured during each of our observation periods. The first panel reflects those measurements we obtained before we lowered the mobile (i.e., two per minute, zero per minute, and one per minute). The second panel reflects those measurements we obtained after we lowered the mobile (i.e., two per minute, eight per minute, and 12 per minute). The solid black lines drawn through the data points in each panel reflect our measure of celeration or the change in rate over time. From the chart, you can

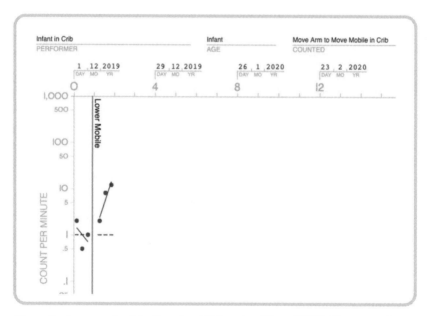

Figure 3. An example of the Standard Celeration Chart (SCC). Rate per minute appears on the vertical axis; successive calendar days appears on the horizontal axis. Each data point reflects rate of arm-moving behavior during each 1-minute observation period. Trend lines through each data series reflect celeration—our index of learning.

see that before we lowered the mobile, the celeration was going down, which we call a deceleration. In other words, the infant's rate of behavior was decreasing or *decelerating* before we lowered the mobile. After we intervened and lowered the mobile, the celeration turned upward and began increasing or *accelerating*.

With our measure of rate plotted on the SCC, we can visually analyze the performance of a learner over time. We have a visual indication of how rapidly behavior is changing or how much learning is taking place. These celerations also produce standard slopes that we can mathematically quantify. That gives us a *quantifiable* index of learning. Moreover, celeration captures the multiplicative nature of learning. As with other natural phenomena, behavior does not add or subtract as it changes. Rather, behavior multiplies when it grows and divides as it decreases.

The standard design of the SCC also enables us to extend celeration lines to predict future performance. Remember that selection by consequences really deals with the future probability of a behavior? Well, Ogden Lindsley's brilliant contribution actually enables us to predict the future course of a behavior.[102]

Going back to the hypothetical SCC I created for our infant, if we extended our celeration line in the first panel—before we lowered the mobile—we can see that our behavior would continue to decelerate. The future path of that celeration predicts that the rate of our infant's arm-moving would continue to decrease, and suggests that our infant is not effectively learning to move their arm to move the mobile. Conversely, if we extend our celeration line in the second panel—after we lowered the mobile—we can predict that the rate of our infant's behavior would continue to accelerate. This indicates that our infant is learning to move their arm in a way that moves the mobile. We are now able to make reliable predictions about learning and future performance—an essential activity for educators.

Learning Is the Result of the Learner's Environment

Let's imagine that those two panels on our hypothetical SCC reflect the performances of two different infants, rather than two different conditions implemented with the same infant. What might a member of the establishments say about those two different infants? The second infant has learned to use their arm to move a mobile above their crib; the first infant has not. Is the first infant disabled, not intelligent, or lazy? Is the second infant gifted, intelligent, or determined? Does classifying these two infants in this way explain the differences in their performance? Absolutely not. One infant simply had the benefit of a learning environment that led to the repeated reinforcement and subsequent learning of a new skill, whereas the other infant did not have the benefit of this kind of learning environment.

Members of the establishments account for learning, or the failure to learn, with hypothetical constructs and explanatory fictions. The outcasts—behavioral scientists like me—account for learning by measuring a learner's behavior over time and adjusting features of the environment to accelerate learning. Our hypothetical infant wasn't learning to use their arm to move the mobile, so we changed the environment to help them learn to do this. Similarly, Alex wasn't learning to read in his school environment because his learning history had failed to produce mastery of component reading skills and had led to the reinforcement and strengthening of habits that interfered with learning those skills. So I changed his environment. I didn't classify him as disabled. I changed his learning environment, and as a result, he learned to read.

With behavioral science, learning becomes something we can precisely define, measure, analyze, understand, and improve. With behavioral science, learning no longer remains an elusive, immeasurable concept attributed to hypothetical inherent causes. Learning as defined becomes learning that is observable and measurable. In this sense, learning becomes the subject matter appropriate to natural science, amenable to its processes and procedures. From science comes pragmatic action. The explanatory fictions of education and psychology have led to systemic educational failure. It is time to bring scientific practices into the classroom as tools with which to analyze and design effective teaching practices.

As educators, behavior is all we can directly access. We cannot see dyslexia; we can only see the behaviors a learner engages in when presented with reading material. We cannot see intelligence; we can only see behaviors individuals engage in that the establishments claim are evidence of intelligence. We cannot see understanding; we can only see a learner behaving effectively with respect to a subject matter. It is behavior we should focus on and behavior we should change to improve the quality of life for an individual. In order to change behavior, we must precisely define, measure, and analyze it over time in relation to those features of the environment that have been discovered by behavioral science to impact learning. Effective educators must act as *scientists*. We need scientists in the classroom just as we need scientists in the operating room. The education of our citizens determines the survival of our species just as much as their medical treatment does. The time to advance beyond prescientific practices in education is upon us. Behavioral science serves as the only means of ending this educational dark age.

Unfortunately, from the establishments' perspective, behavior is not important. Behavior is seen as a byproduct of the more important subject matter for educators: mental activity or the metaphysical aspect of students. Thus, in traditional education, behavior is ignored, and the learning process misunderstood. Next, we'll see how educational practices are based on traditions and myths, which have no basis in how human beings actually learn. To the contrary, the design of our schools stems from how the establishments *believe* children learn. These beliefs have led to ineffective educational traditions and, as a result, myths have been invented to excuse the systemic failure of our schools.

4

THE TRADITIONS

"The language of modern Education, which has been aptly called Educanto, can reduce any mildly sensitive layman to a state of helpless fury in a matter of minutes."
—JAMES KOERNER[6]

I have observed a lot of classrooms throughout my career, and the scene is typically the same. The class period often starts with the teacher returning papers that have been graded for an assignment that was completed many days before. Some students seem pleased about their grades; however, many look forlorn, slump down further in their seats, avert their eyes and quickly hide the graded assignment. Watching kids respond to the grades they receive can be a truly heartbreaking experience.

After papers are returned, the teacher typically stands in front of the class and starts talking. Some students in the class have their eyes trained on the teacher, seemingly paying attention to the lesson. However, a majority of the students aren't looking at the teacher but are doing other things like looking at one another, picking their fingernails, doodling, staring out the window, or sleeping. When the teacher eventually asks a question of the class, a few alert students raise their hands to answer. Unfortunately, an overwhelming majority of students do not raise their hands. The lucky student who gets called on has the opportunity to respond and receive feedback from the teacher. The rest of the class does not. On a single day in the same class, students have vastly different experiences.

Even for those students who do appear to be paying attention to the lesson, it is difficult to determine if learning is actually occurring. A student may have their eyes on the teacher, but it is highly likely that they are thinking about things other than the lesson at hand. Since very few students actually participate, it is difficult to determine who is learning and who isn't.

Eventually, the bell rings, students move on to another class period, and the cycle repeats itself. I always find it extraordinary that during a class period, the person who has behaved the most with respect to the subject matter to be learned is the teacher, *not* the students. When the students file past me to their next activity or class period, I always get this sinking feeling that another hour of these children's lives has just been wasted. I have no idea if any of them have learned anything because very few actually said or did anything meaningful during the entire class period. Most of them just sat at their desks staring blankly.

A majority of students move mindlessly through their school day because of the traditions that dominate our nation's schools. At this point, you have met the establishments and, hopefully, have a greater understanding of how our entrenched belief systems have given rise to their existence and continued dominance in our culture. You have also met the outcasts: the behavioral scientists who have been historically excluded from the establishments. Now we must deal with the traditions practiced by the establishments as a result of our culture's entrenched beliefs.

Educational traditions arise from blind spots regarding how learning actually occurs. Let's be clear from the start that these traditions don't exist because they work. They exist because people *believe* in them and, more important, because it's just how we've always done things. More often than not, traditions continue because we think we don't have a choice. We become so blind to these traditions that we never consider other options. Traditions are just as dangerous and difficult to change as the establishments that give rise to them.

STUDENTS MUST RAISE THEIR HANDS

In a majority of our nation's schools, class participation requires that students *raise their hands*. I have absolutely no idea when this tradition first began, but I assume that it has been in practice since the dawn of formal education. When one imagines students in a classroom, one envisions students sitting at their desks with their hands raised. In the romantic version, all students will have their eyes intensely trained on the teacher with all of their hands eagerly raised in hopes of being the lucky one chosen to answer whatever question has been presented to the class. Unfortunately, as I just described, the more realistic picture entails a few students with their hands up, a few sleeping, a few doodling, a few whispering, a few staring into space, a few looking in their desks, a few picking their fingernails, and so on.

The tradition of *hand-raising* is one of the most telling indications that the educational establishment has no idea how learning actually takes place. As a behavioral scientist, I am absolutely shocked that the establishment expects all students in a class to learn when only the lucky few are provided the opportunity to respond and have that response reinforced. An entire century of science has led to the discovery that learning occurs, and only occurs, when behavior is consistently reinforced over time. The tradition of hand-raising may be the single most detrimental practice employed by our nation's schools. As I will discuss in detail, it has been scientifically determined that effective instruction requires *choral responding* where the entire class responds in unison to questions or prompts presented by the teacher with feedback immediately provided to the entire class.[104]

Not only does choral responding create the opportunity for reinforcement of that responding for every student in the class, it also encourages and strengthens class engagement. When an entire class of students is required to respond to every question a teacher presents, each student's attention is reinforced along with the actual response to the lesson. The teacher can also quickly identify when the class struggles to answer, which alerts her that she may have failed to present the question clearly or that her class requires further clarification of the concept. Then she can immediately adjust her instruction by rephrasing the question, breaking the concept down into smaller units, or providing a prompt or model to promote correct responding by the class.

A majority of students basically sleep through their school day. Only a few show up to school with the desire to participate. Most students therefore are failing to learn the lessons. The establishments lead us to admire the students who participate and blame the ones who don't. However, those who participate are lucky enough to have learning histories that established that repertoire. Those students who do not readily participate have learning histories that failed to establish that repertoire. It is the responsibility of schools to educate all students, even those with unfortunate learning histories. By requiring and, most important, reinforcing choral responding by the entire class, a teacher can ensure that all students engage, participate, and learn the lesson — not just the few who show up to class eager to learn. To be frank, it is the students who do not show up that way who require the most from their schools.

CONTENT EMPHASIZED OVER COMPETENCY

Due to blind spots about the learning process, the educational establishment asserts that the key to improving educational outcomes is to expose students to more and more content in earlier and earlier grades. From their perspective, learning is simply providing students with experiences, so the sooner students have experience with complex subject matter, the better. So we have kindergartners expected to write about their day and first graders expected to solve math word problems, even though kindergartners are just learning to identify and write letters, and first graders are just learning how to read and add. The establishment presents their ideologies in a way that is very appealing to the public — a romantic vision that kindergartners should be writing prose and first graders performing logical problem-solving. However, as I hope you all now recognize, this romantic vision translates into an ugly reality. The nature of human learning, which has been scientifically determined, necessitates that complex repertoires are broken down into component skills and that these component skills are systematically and repeatedly practiced until mastery occurs. In other words, we must learn, and master, *first things first.*

Not only is the *first things first* mantra common sense, it is a scientifically proven fact about learning regardless of the skill being learned. One cannot master tennis unless grip, stance, ball position, racket placement, racket speed, footwork, and timing are separately practiced to mastery. Similarly, one cannot effectively perform algebra without mastery of basic numeracy and computation skills. The majority of the world understands this reality with respect to mastering a sport, a musical instrument, or a game like chess. However, the establishment has done such a brilliant job selling the progressive ideology that common sense has been replaced with irrational and erroneous ideas about how children learn academic skills. The NAEP results indicate the grim reality of what progressive education actually produces: A majority of American students who cannot read, write, think critically, or do math. Just because we like the idea of very young learners performing highly complex academic and cognitive skills does not also mean that young learners will be able to learn and master such skills. I like the idea of snapping my fingers and having a million dollars appear in my bank account. I think we all know the likelihood of such a thing actually happening. For most logical humans, there is a clear difference between fantasy and reality; however, when it comes to American education, fantasy and reality have become quite blurred.

Fit Learning, along with other organizations informed by behavioral science, has systematically identified the essential foundational skills that students must learn and master before being able to successfully move up a curriculum ladder. We have also demonstrated that when students are allowed the time required to learn and master the basics, more complex skills emerge automatically with little to no training. Instead, the establishment wants educators to skip the basic steps and spend their time exposing students to the complex skills at the top of a curriculum ladder. I understand the appeal of the fantasy. Who wants to spend the time and energy required for kids to master the basics when you can just skip over all of that laborious, boring stuff and focus on what educators find more interesting? However, the goal of education should not be about satisfying the interests and opinions of educators. It should be about effectively educating kids.

CURRICULUM CONFUSED WITH INSTRUCTION

Another blind spot exists regarding what instruction actually entails. The educational establishment touts its "pedagogical" expertise and actively isolates teachers from the rest of the scholarly and intellectual world. When undergraduate college students decide to major in education, they effectively stop taking classes from anyone other than professional educators. History, math, or science courses for teachers in training are not taught by the scholars and experts in these fields, but rather by professional educators who present their own pedagogical versions of these disciplines. Moreover, professors in colleges of education and their students do not participate in the critical discourse and peer-reviewed scholarly activities of faculty and students in the other disciplines. Such isolation has resulted in dogmatic, uncontested, and intractable traditions within teacher training programs, and thus, education as a whole.

Although the educational establishment declares pedagogy as its discipline and expertise, it is profoundly unclear what pedagogy actually means from their perspective. As defined, pedagogy means *the study and practice of teaching as an academic or theoretical concept.* However, the establishment cannot operationally define what "good" teaching entails, objectively measure what types of instructional behaviors reflect "good" teaching, link objective measures of instruction with student outcomes, or consistently train "good" teachers. The establishment does not seem to have a firm grasp of what they are supposed to be training teachers to do or how to train them to do it. More often than not, good teaching is seen as a matter of talent where some people *have it* and others do not. It seems like the goal of teacher training programs is simply to discover the talented teachers. We have a large population of children to educate. We need to be producing well-trained, effective teachers, not waiting for them to magically appear or be discovered.

Much of what teachers learn during their training involves various theories regarding what children should learn and how they should learn it. Pedagogy represents an idea, not a system of empirically validated teaching practices proven to produce effective outcomes with students. Again, the educational establishment exists as an ideological institution, not a pragmatic one. From their perspective, there is no one correct teaching method and the notion that there might be is absolute blasphemy! Teaching is perceived as an art, not a science. Throughout their training, teachers learn "methods" that reflect various theories or ideas about what curriculum to use and how to go about teaching it. Ultimately, it is up to the teacher to choose the method that they think works best.

Let's step back for a moment and imagine if engineering functioned this way. Imagine that, rather than the physical sciences, engineers were trained in various theories about how bridges work and how to construct them. After those theories are offered, engineers are left to decide for themselves how they want to design and build a bridge. We can all imagine the result of such training. Many bridges would fail, and many people would die! Yet all of our teachers are trained this way, and we want to hold them accountable when students fail. Would we hold engineers accountable for a bridge collapsing if the establishments refused to properly educate them in the physical sciences? How can we possibly expect teachers to effectively educate children when the establishment refuses to provide them with the training required? The entire notion is ludicrous! Along with students, teachers are tragic victims of the establishment. They are thrown to the wolves every day, expected to use theories, magic, and talent to properly educate our nation's youth. Teachers deserve better.

The educational establishment also confuses curriculum with instruction. Curriculum entails the *what*—what materials are presented or what is to be learned. Instruction involves the *how* and is the most critical determinant of learning. Instruction involves how curriculum materials are presented; how complex content is broken down into smaller, learnable units; how feedback is provided; how prompts are delivered and how such prompts are effectively removed; how learning is measured; and how mastery is determined. It is the *how* that determines whether students learn and master *what* is to be learned. Effective instruction involves understanding both—the how and the what.

Even the *what* of education proves problematic. Most of the time, curriculum materials are published by large companies that employ professional educators, rather than scholars in a field, to design the content.[6] This creates a twofold issue: Teachers are neither effectively trained in instruction—in *how* learning occurs—nor are they provided with materials designed by experts in the content area being instructed.

The *how* of instruction also greatly impacts the design of curriculum. Being an expert in a particular content area does not automatically translate into expertise in how to teach it. The Technology of Teaching, which I will describe in detail shortly, entails the logical analysis of curriculum in such a way that its presentation leads to student learning and mastery. Instructional design is not the same as curriculum content. Curriculum content should be produced by biologists, historians, mathematicians, linguists, and so forth. The scholars in these fields should inform educators about the essential content of those disciplines. However, how that content is designed, sequenced, and instructed should be determined by behavioral science, which has led to a scientific understanding of how to program instruction so that learning and mastery reliably occurs.

GRADE LEVEL ADVANCEMENT

As I've mentioned, developmental theories have dominated education for over a century. The psychological establishment has led people to believe that children acquire skills according to stages and, like plants, simply require nutrients and an enriched environment in order to proceed through them. It is undeniable that physical growth does follow a predictable pattern largely determined by our genetic endowment. However, a big leap is made when the learning of *skills* is also attributed to predestined stages of growth and failure to learn attributed to immaturity or a slower progression through developmental stages. Learning skills does not naturally happen as a function of age. The brain does not unfold over time in such a way that children can suddenly begin engaging in skills they were never previously able to perform. Children do not spontaneously start reading or doing math because they turned six and the reading and math skills stored in their brains were suddenly unlocked and allowed to unfold. This notion is categorically false.

As I have explained, children learn skills through very specific interactions with their environments. Such skills are gradually shaped over time starting with smaller approximations of a skill and gradually moving toward the more complex repertoire as each smaller component is practiced, reinforced, and strengthened. More often than not, this type of shaping occurs by accident through common sense parenting or teaching practices. It can *appear* as if new skills spontaneously emerge as a function of age because the selecting and strengthening features of a child's environment are undetectable to the layperson. However, that the causal variables for a child's learning are not detectable or understandable does not imply that these selecting variables are not occurring. Because they are not understood, these critical features of learning environments are often left to chance.

Due to the influence of the psychological establishment in education, children advance from grade to grade based on age rather than on mastery of the prerequisite skills. Children move from kindergarten to first grade because they turn six, not because they have mastered identifying letters, identifying phonics sounds, and decoding basic phonetic words and are ready to begin learning the higher-level reading skills traditionally targeted in first grade. It is assumed that, because they are a year older, they are ready for higher-level skills. Again, this misunderstanding has tragic implications for education. Children do not master skills based on physical growth as they age. Children master skills as a result of repeated reinforced practice of such skills to a level of automaticity synonymous with neurological permanence. We call this *fluency*—automatic, effortless, neurologically permanent skills available for the learning of more complex skills.[105]

Schools do not provide the type of training that produces fluency with learners. On the contrary, practice in the classroom is actively discouraged by the educational establishment. Teachers are trained to believe that drill and practice suppresses discovery and creativity—though no scientific evidence exists to support this notion. As a result, students are pushed along through the grade levels regardless of their prerequisite skill mastery and resulting ability to successfully learn and master the skills expected in each subsequent grade. The NAEP data indicate that students do not perform better simply as a function of age, maturation, or time, and support the assertion that grade-level advancement based on age rather than prerequisite skill mastery is scientifically contraindicated and tragically ineffective.

GRADING PRACTICES AND STANDARDIZED TESTS

Grades serve as the primary means of evaluating learning in education. Behavioral science has led to the discovery that celeration, or change in rate over time, is the most sensitive and reliable measure of learning. There are standard measures of health used in medicine, such as body temperature, heartbeats per minute, and respirations per minute. Similarly, there are standard measures of behavior and learning: rate and celeration. Rate and celeration allow for the analysis of whether or not learning is occurring, how fast learning is occurring, and whether or not a skill has been mastered. Grades are a measure of performance—not a measure of the actual learning process. We can understand nothing about learning by measuring a skill once, which is what traditional grading practices entail. We can only understand learning by measuring behavior over time. Learning is a process — it occurs through time and takes time to occur, and it should be measured as such.

Moreover, grades are an insensitive, unreliable measure of performance that are not based on scientifically valid measures of behavior and learning. Grades are an educational tradition guided by belief, not a practice established through the scientific process. Unlike rate and celeration, grades do not predict that a skill is truly mastered such that it is neurologically permanent (i.e., remembered), resistant to distractions and fatigue, and usable for the learning of more complex skills. Grades are not scientific measures of learning — rate and celeration are scientific measures of learning.

To make matters worse, in many schools, traditional letter-grading practices often do not emerge until 3rd or even 6th grade. In these cases, subjective evaluation practices are the primary means of monitoring and communicating student progress. Some schools implement an arbitrary numbering system or, in more disturbing cases, a progression of faces that go from happy to increasingly sad along some arbitrary scale. Obviously, neither method reflects an objective, standard measure of performance and none have been empirically validated as reliable measures of learning. It has been demonstrated that personality, physical appearance, socioeconomic status, race, gender, or a learning disability label can influence a teacher's subjective evaluation of student performance. As I will argue in Chapter 6, although traditional letter-grading practices can be more objective and linked to a measurable standard like percent correct, even letter grades do not reflect empirically validated measures of learning.

Grading practices in education also result in delayed feedback. Typically, students complete a test or assignment, turn it in, and must wait for the teacher to grade and return it. But immediate reinforcement is a critical determinant of learning. Receiving feedback on a test or assignment days or even weeks after it was completed can have little to no impact on future performance. Moreover, grades must actually serve as reinforcing consequences for academic behavior to be strengthened, which is sadly not the case for many students who have only experienced academic failure and low grades. More often than not, grades function as a punishing or aversive consequence, which often produce emotional responding and a tendency to escape or avoid academic environments altogether.

Grades are also often viewed as reflections of inherent characteristics of the student. If a student gets an A, they are considered smart, hard-working, or talented. If a student gets an F, they are considered stupid, lazy, or disabled. Rather than being an evaluation of the learning environment and effectiveness of the instruction, grades are seen as an indication of inherent ability, or inability for that matter. Students receive the grade and the teacher moves on regardless of how the student actually performed. Teaching practices are not adjusted, and learning is not continually evaluated so that actual mastery of the material is achieved. Students are expected to learn the material the way the material is presented, according to the timeline set by the establishment. Such grading and teaching practices are a direct contradiction to the "student-centered" practices touted by the educational establishment—what occurs in reality is quite different from what is romanticized in theory. Despite the progressive rhetoric, students are expected to learn in the same way and at the same pace, and failure is attributed to some intrinsic flaw rather than to faulty instructional practices.

As I have stated, traditional grading systems do not reflect empirically validated measures of learning. In other words, an A does not effectively predict that a skill is permanently learned or usable for learning more complex skills. Many parents, including myself, can anecdotally report instances in which their children received an A on a test but could not recall any of the tested information even a week later. Our culture is grade-obsessed, and most parents dream of their children being straight A students. However, if we cannot trust that an A is a valid measure of learning, what is the point? Of course, there are students who receive A grades and do permanently learn the material. But this permanent learning was not produced by the A grade. It was produced by the manner in which these students studied.

As I have said, learning is a process. Consistently practicing, rehearsing, or studying academic material *over time* produces permanent learning outcomes, not grades. Many students cram for a test the night before and can score an A; however, cramming does not produce neurological permanence of skills and content. Such skills or content are available for only a short period of time before being forgotten. There are also those learners who do engage in consistent practice of material and do not achieve As for a number of reasons. Poorly designed tests or barrier behaviors that arise during testing situations can all lead to poor test performance, despite the fact that a student has actually learned some or all of the material.

In addition to grades, standardized tests are also administered once per year, typically toward the end of the year, as a means of evaluating student progress towards grade-level standards. Because such tests are often administered in the spring, little time remains to take action with students who perform poorly. As a result, failing students finish the school year behind only to enter the next grade the following year already significantly behind.

In addition to test scores being reported without time for intervention, such scores also provide little information regarding specific skill deficits. Standardized tests are not prescriptive. They do not provide for the precise identification of skills deficits so that effective skill-building programs can be designed. In contrast, standardized tests provide one score for large, aggregate academic domains that involve hundreds of individual, component skills. It is not possible for teachers to decipher from a standardized test score what aspect of the complex repertoire might be deficient.

More important, standardized tests are often treated *descriptively* rather than prescriptively. The establishment tends to view such tests as a means of describing the inherent abilities of students, not evaluating instructional practices to determine if they are effective or need to be changed. Standardized tests are rarely considered an evaluation of the instruction. They are typically seen as an evaluation of the student. The psychological establishment has led us to believe that tests like these measure inherent characteristics or traits that are largely fixed or unchangeable.

Standardized test scores lead to normal distributions where the lucky few with effective learning histories score in the high "tail," the large majority of mediocritized students score under the "bell," and the more tragically failed learners score in the "low" tail of the distribution. The psychological establishment has led us to believe that distributions of this sort are "normal." From their perspective, these distributions reflect the nature of human variation in aptitude. Later, I will provide evidence that these distributions are not fixed, and they most certainly do not reflect ability. These tests and their corresponding distributions simply reflect the performance of skills that must be learned via effective instruction and repeated, reinforced practice. These tests provide no information as to why a small percentage of students perform well or why a large majority of students' performances are mediocre or poor. These tests simply reflect the performance. The answer to the question of why students perform in particular ways lies in the analysis of those students' individual learning histories and, more important, the type of instructional practices being used.

IMMEASURABLE GOALS AND OBJECTIVES

Most educational goals and objectives entail descriptions that cannot possibly be measured. Just visit any state Department of Education website and follow the links for state standards to determine the veracity of this statement. Here are a few from New York State (nysed.gov):

> *"Demonstrate command of the conventions of academic English grammar and usage when writing or speaking."*
>
> *"Apply knowledge of language to understand how language functions in different contexts to make effective choices for meaning or style, and to comprehend more fully when reading or listening."*
>
> *"Make sense of problems and persevere in solving them."*
>
> *"Reason abstractly and quantitatively."*

One need not be a scientist to quickly recognize the absurdity of these statements. How might one measure a "demonstration" or "command" of something? How does one measure "applying knowledge" or "understanding" or "making effective choices"? How does one measure "making sense of" or "persevering"? How does one measure "reasoning"?

These objectives reflect the ideology of the educational establishment, which does not translate into the practical matter of designing effective instruction and measuring the effects of that instruction to ensure that learning and mastery has occurred. These objectives reflect *ideas* about the goals of education. However, how is a teacher to possibly know if and when such objectives have been accomplished? Just as the objectives reflect ideas, the evaluation of whether such objectives have actually been accomplished also remains theoretical. It is assumed that, if the establishment puts forth these very erudite objectives, teachers will provide opportunities for students to learn them.

In order for education to accomplish pragmatic goals, such goals must be measurable. Otherwise, we are forced to remain in an imaginary world of lofty ideologies and theoretical learning outcomes. That is the educational world we have been living in, which has produced over 80 years of educational failure. Rather than referring to hypothetical constructs like "command of," "making sense of," "understanding," or "comprehending," we must construct objectives based on what learners are to *do*, how well they must *do it*, and how we are to measure their *doing of it*. For example, here is a measurable objective for English grammar that we use at Fit Learning:

> *"Students will see and mark the subject of each sentence at 30 correct marks and 1 error or less per minute."*

Now we have a goal that is measurable, so that the teacher can know when the objective has actually been achieved. It is actually quite simple. But we have a romanticized ideology that sounds very impressive and appealing to the public. Who wouldn't want their child to "reason abstractly and quantitatively"? However, we have to resist the attractiveness of these ideological goals in favor of pragmatic ones if education is ever going to improve.

The establishment has been putting forth goals and objectives in this kind of "Educanto" for more than a century.[6] The lofty, verbose, and obtuse language of the educational establishment leads to a kind of confusion that prevents the public from questioning what any of it actually means. This "Educanto" has the flavor of scientific language leading the public to assume it must be valid.[6] However, no one actually understands it, especially the teachers who are ultimately responsible for ensuring that these illusive objectives are achieved. Again, we have teachers as tragic victims of the establishment and their corresponding traditions.

THE VICIOUS CYCLE OF SCHOOL FAILURE

As I hope you now understand, schools aren't designed according to the science of human learning. Schools are designed according to traditions and beliefs. The educational establishment *believes* that students learn via exposure to experiences, so a majority of the school day involves teachers doing a lot of talking and students doing a lot of staring, sleeping, fidgeting, or daydreaming. The establishment believes that teachers must simply *expose* students to the opportunity to learn things. Whether or not things actually get learned is seen as the student's responsibility. How the learning process actually occurs is completely misunderstood in education.

The establishment sets an arbitrary timeline that teachers and students are expected to follow. Thus, students spend a predetermined amount of time on a particular lesson, get tested on that lesson, receive a grade of some sort, and are pushed on to the next lesson—regardless of the grade received. Grades are viewed as an evaluation of the student, not an evaluation of the instruction. Students are expected to raise their hands, sit quietly and attentively in class, and make good grades. When students fail to do these things, that failure is attributed to problems inherent to the student.

The beliefs and traditions that dominate our schools are *never* called into question. So, the cycle of systemic academic failure repeats itself year after year and student after student. What will it take to put an end to this cycle? What will it take for the public to declare that enough is enough? I'm hoping that uncovering your blind spots regarding how learning actually occurs might be the tipping point. I'm hoping that these distinctions might lead you all to feel as outraged as I do. Educational practices should be based on how learning *actually* occurs, not on how the establishment *believes* learning occurs.

5

THE MYTHS

*"Science thrives on errors, cutting them away one by one. . . .
Pseudoscience is just the opposite. Hypotheses are often framed
precisely so they are invulnerable to any experiment that offers a
prospect of disproof, so even in principle they cannot be invalidated."*
—CARL SAGAN[64]

As I stated in the introduction, one of the most reward-ing experiences throughout my career has been help-ing parents discover their blind spots. I'll never forget when Alex's mom had that breakthrough moment about the real reason he hadn't learned to read. When a parent suddenly gets it — has that "aha" moment — it's a very powerful experience. When Alex's mom had her moment, it evoked laughter, tears, and a little bit of rage. She couldn't believe that a problem that had previously seemed completely unsolvable actually had such a simple explanation and solution. Alex hadn't mastered essential tool skills for reading and had developed some bad habits instead. He simply needed repeated, reinforced practice of skills to mastery and he needed immediate corrective feedback on his bad reading habits.

Alex's mom was mind-blown at how simple the answer was and that I provided her with evidence of his progress every step of the way. She had never personally experienced the life-changing process of science before. Most people don't realize how deeply human and loving science actually is. Science can seem cold and scary. However, the application of behavioral science to the education of children is a profoundly humane approach guided by love and a commitment to the transformation of a child's life. Tears, hugs, joy, and amazement define the experience of our learners and parents. We may be doing science, but from their perspective, we make miracles happen on a daily basis.

Like Alex's mom, many of you reading this book have probably been through the ringer with your kids, spending your time and money on endless evaluations or services that make absolutely no difference. You have been told to follow this frustrating path by people who present themselves as the "experts." Unfortunately, the recommendations made by these so-called experts are largely based on myths.

Now that we have taken on the establishments and their corresponding traditions, let's address the myths about learning that dominate our culture. These myths have also arisen from the establishments and reflect the various reasons that have been invented to excuse the systemic failures of our schools. The myths I am going to describe do not originate from any kind of scientific evidence. Rather, they have been invented as a means of explaining away the accumulating evidence that, more often than not, the traditions put forth by the establishments don't work.

MYTH #1: ALL KIDS LEARN DIFFERENTLY

I hope I have now demonstrated that this statement is categorically false. There are fundamental principles of learning that have been discovered through the natural science of behavior. All kids *do not* learn differently. The learning process is the same across all learners regardless of age, disability, label, gender, socioeconomic status, race, or ethnicity. The learning process is the same regardless of the skill being learned: sports, musical instruments, academic subjects, fine motor skills, gross motor skills, verbal skills, adaptive skills, or sadly, maladaptive skills. We have evolved as a species to learn through specific interactions with our environment.

The natural science of behavior has discovered that learning occurs through the repeated reinforcement of behavior over time. The more often a behavior occurs and is reinforced, the stronger that behavior becomes, until eventually it is established as a permanent part of a person's repertoire. All humans learn this way. Moreover, reinforcement of behavior is happening whether we know it or not. Unfortunately, more often than not, people do not understand this principle, and students are not given intentional opportunities to practice a desirable behavior so that it can be repeatedly reinforced and become permanent. When learning environments are poorly designed or left to chance, the result is chaos. This accounts for the many frustrations people experience as teachers or parents. When a child's environment occurs without *intentional* design, problematic behavioral repertoires are often reinforced and strengthened by accident at the expense of the strengthening of more desirable behaviors.

The result of this disastrous state of affairs is obvious from our nation's NAEP scores, the increasing prevalence of learning disability diagnoses, and the number of disciplinary referrals by teachers. Of course, it is not only teachers who require training in the intentional design of learning environments; parents must learn how to do this too. More often than not, maladaptive behavior starts at home, but is often exacerbated or promulgated by ineffective school environments.

When the role of the environment is ignored or misunderstood, the only thing left to do is explain away academic failures or maladaptive behaviors with hypothetical constructs such as learning disabilities, personality characteristics, or other traits assumed to be inherent to the individual. It is much easier to make up mythological causes for problems than it is to do the actual analysis of the true origins of those problems. Trust me, behavioral science may be pragmatic and involve simple explanations and solutions, but it is not easy. It requires a willingness to be fully responsible for learning along with a rigorous adherence to the process of natural science. From this perspective, I can understand the great resistance to its adoption. However, is effectively treating cancer, building bridges, or designing clean energy easy? I would suggest that educating our children should be not about what is easy but rather about what is effective. Imagine what kind of world we would live in if we did only what was easy.

The statement I made earlier that the learning process is the same across all learners requires clarification. This is not to imply that all learners will be able to learn the same skill, at the same pace, with the same reinforcers. Behavioral science is the *science of individual differences*. Although the process by which we learn is the same, individual learners have their own unique genetic endowments and learning histories. This individual learning history requires careful analysis and understanding. For example, learners have unique preferences that influence what types of consequences will actually function as reinforcers and strengthen behavior. Learners also have different component skill repertoires that might enhance or interfere with learning a new skill. Similarly, learners engage in different types of maladaptive behaviors that must be understood in terms of their behavioral history and how these barriers were established in the first place.

Behavioral scientists act as *historians of the individual*. We must analyze learners' current behavioral repertoires with respect to their individual learning histories in order to design effective, individualized teaching practices. What is individualized involves the type of skill being trained, the types of prompts required to promote a correct response, the kind of reinforcers used, and the manner in which barrier behaviors are addressed, which is based upon the history of reinforcement that led to the establishment of those behaviors in the first place. What is *not* individualized is the actual learning process, which dictates that all learners must frequently behave in the desired way and that behavior must be repeatedly reinforced over time in order for learning to occur.

MYTH #2: WE SHOULD TEACH TO A CHILD'S STRENGTHS

It is hard for me to count the number of times I have heard members of the establishments make this statement, and it is one of the more infuriating learning myths. Getting children to do what they already know how to do is easy. It is getting children to learn and master what they *do not* know how to do that is the challenge. Is the goal of education to have kids learn only what they find easy? Actually, that appears to be the case if our NAEP scores are any indication. However, I would say that the goal of education is to produce expertise across all disciplines such that all learners can achieve greatness in their lives and make profound contributions to the world. This goal cannot be achieved by teaching kids only what they find easy to learn. We should actually be teaching to a child's weaknesses, not strengths. However, teaching children to learn and master difficult things requires expertise in learning and instruction guided by behavioral science. Since few teachers have access to the training required for such expertise, it becomes clear why the myth of teaching to a child's strengths evolved in the first place. Due to their insufficient training, teachers have no other option.

More often than not, this myth revolves around the sensory modality used in learning. It is commonplace to hear children categorized as auditory or visual learners, but these categorizations are completely false. We do not learn through a process similar to osmosis where information passes through our eyes or ears and into our brains. So when people make statements about auditory or visual learners, they are actually referring to how a learner behaves with respect to auditory or visual materials — in other words, *what* children need to learn how to respond to. Again, we have curriculum being confused with learning. Some children may respond more effectively to auditory materials and others may respond better to visual materials. However, these differences have nothing to do with their being auditory or visual learners. These differences have to do with the fact that, for whatever reason, their individual learning histories have produced better *listening* skills than *looking* skills or vice versa.

We take for granted that, because children have eyes and ears, they will *look* and *listen*. This notion is also tragically false. Seeing and hearing are biological abilities. Looking and listening are skills, and like any skill, they require training through repeated practice and reinforcement. If learners do not respond well to auditory materials, then they likely need training to be better *listeners*. Similarly, if learners do not respond well to visual materials, then they likely need training to be better *lookers*. Unfortunately, the establishment has ensured that teachers do not understand this issue and, more often than not, many learners eventually receive mythical learning disability diagnoses as a result of deficient looking and listening skills that are never strengthened through effective training.

The notion that some children are concrete learners and will always require tangibles when learning is also infuriating. As I have described, all children must first learn things that have concrete correspondence in the world before moving into the abstract. Children do not learn to speak by conjugating verbs. They first learn to name concrete things in the world. Similarly, children learn to count tangibles before they can free count, compute with tangibles before doing mental math, and copy words before free-writing words. So to assert that some children learn better with tangible or concrete stimuli is to imply that there are those children who do not require this step. All children must learn to respond to concrete, tangible stimuli in the world before learning to respond to abstract stimuli. The false statement that some children must always learn with tangibles is based on poorly designed teaching practices. What it really means is that teachers have not been trained to effectively shape a learner from the concrete to the abstract. This myth has everything to do with ineffective teaching practices and nothing to do with some inherent characteristic of the learner.

MYTH #3: THEY'RE JUST NOT READY YET

This myth is a classic statement made to parents of early elementary age children who fail to adequately progress in academic areas. Due to the influence of the psychological establishment, teachers are led to believe that children acquire academic skills as a function of their development rather than as a result of effective instruction.

Obviously there are aspects of physical development required before a child can successfully learn certain things. However, once a child begins talking and learning skills in the natural environment, which for most begins in toddlerhood, they are capable of learning just about anything if it is properly sequenced, instructed, practiced, and reinforced. We are not *born* with the ability to read or do math. We must *learn* these things as they are human inventions passed down via instruction, not genetics. If a child fails to adequately learn to read during 1st grade, turning a year older is not going to change anything.

To the contrary, the longer children fail to succeed academically, the more likely it is that these skills deficits become harder to fix. Children do not read because they are ready. They read because they have learned to do so through effective instruction.

MYTH #4: THEY'RE JUST NOT GOOD AT IT

By far the most common myth is the notion of inherent talent. *Some kids are just bad at math. Some kids are just bad readers or writers.* That we so easily accept such statements speaks volumes regarding our entrenched belief in *talent* as a causal factor. It also speaks volumes to the fact that we have basically given up on the idea that education is responsible for effectively educating all kids. In other words, what is being declared is that education works for the lucky, talented few, and we just have to accept that.

As a behavioral scientist who has dramatically accelerated the academic skills of thousands of even the most challenged students, I vehemently reject the notion of inherent talent as the cause of academic success or failure. First and foremost, this view is just plain lazy and discourages effective action. Second, it resembles Social Darwinism, where the failures of economically and socially disadvantaged groups are falsely justified by reference to supposed genetic inferiority.[18] Absolutely no empirical evidence supports such notions. Privileged white people are not genetically superior to other groups. They just have access to more resources and always have had. Third, as I've mentioned, academic skills are not genetically determined. People are not born with inherited math or reading abilities. Academic skills are acquired based on training, not inheritance.

Because members of the establishment are unaware of the specific features of the environment responsible for learning, mythical explanations for success or failure must be invented. As a result, the lucky few with effective learning histories successfully acquire expertise in complex skills, and the remaining majority do not. Those lucky few are described as *talented* and the remainder as *not talented*. However, with behavioral science, it is possible to intentionally design learning environments so that a majority of learners acquire expertise in complex skills, not just the lucky few. To accomplish the goal of effectively educating all learners, we must reject explanatory fictions such as talent or inherent ability. We must commit to understanding academic failure as a function of a learner's current and past academic environment and corresponding learning history. We must also commit to the intentional design of learning environments based on the principles of learning offered by behavioral science.

The counterpoint to the fiction of attributing failure to learning disabilities is the fiction of attributing success to talent. What leads us to describe someone as having talent or being talented? As with a learner diagnosed with dyslexia, someone is described as having talent based on what we see them *doing*. Again, from this perspective, talent is a *doing* not a *having*. Talented musicians are admired for how they play their instruments, talented athletes for how they play their sport, talented chefs for how they cook, talented writers for how they write. In each of these examples, we declare someone talented based on their behavior or what we see them *do*. We cannot see talent; we can only observe the behavior of those we call talented. In other words, talent is behavior—or, more specifically, talent is behavior that we might describe as fluent, high-quality, and effortless. Talent is synonymous with the behavior of an expert, and expertise is learned through a very specific type of training and practice. Expertise is behavior that has been learned to *mastery*. Fit Learning has been producing fluent, expert performers in academic subjects for 20 years, and most of these performers were initially low-performing and unmotivated. None of our learners achieved their expertise as a result of talent. This expertise was achieved through the type of instruction and training afforded by behavioral science.

If we are to solve the many problems facing the human race, we must produce *experts*. We must design learning environments that produce what we call *talent*. Our educational system is based on admiring the talented few and inventing mythical explanations for the failures of the majority. The tragic result of this system is reflected by the fact that less than 10% of American students graduate from high school at the advanced level in any academic subject.[1] We are certainly not producing a significant number of experts who can solve the world's crises. However, the natural science of behavior *exists*. The means by which instruction can be systematically designed for the success of every student *exist*. The means for identifying the actual causes for academic failure and success *exist*. The scientific tools required to design teaching practices so that the majority of students graduate as experts *exist*. In short, a Technology of Teaching *exists*. It is time for all of us to demand that this science be acknowledged and implemented by the establishment. We would not tolerate the failure of the medical establishment to implement life-saving practices discovered by medical science. We should no longer tolerate this same failure by the educational establishment.

MYTH #5: CURRICULUM MATERIALS MUST CAPTURE STUDENT INTEREST

When the variables that determine learning are not understood, the establishment is left grasping at straws. Hence, the myth that in order for learners to effectively engage with academic material, that material must be designed to *catch their interest*. This is evidenced by the ridiculous design of most curriculum materials, particularly for young learners. Pick up any workbook, worksheet, or textbook and see how many cartoon characters, hearts, balloons, stars, happy faces, and silly mottos you can count on one page. I promise, you will find more of that stuff than you will the content that must actually be learned.

The theory is that you can trick students into learning if you cover their academic materials with silly images. I cannot overemphasize the absurdity of this myth. Children do not learn better when their materials are illustrated with cartoon characters or balloons. On the contrary, this nonsense distracts learners from what they should actually be paying attention to.

At Fit Learning, we design all of our materials with as few distractions and as many learning opportunities as possible. You will see an example of a piece of our curriculum below, which we use to build fluency in phonics with all of our learners regardless of their age. We use the same materials with our 3-year-olds as we do with our adult learners.

You will not find a single cartoon character or other silly image on any piece of curriculum in our library, which includes hundreds

fit learning™

TITLE:	Phonemic Awareness Sequence/ Consonants									
AIM:	80+ sounds/min									
f	b	h	w	d	h	j	t	j	c	*10*
n	r	g	g	n	t	y	s	w	g	*20*
m	z	w	v	s	v	x	c	p	v	*30*
y	f	s	z	d	y	l	b	y	h	*40*
x	b	h	j	g	b	m	w	p	l	*50*
m	t	p	c	r	y	z	c	r	n	*60*
z	k	r	g	f	k	k	x	j	g	*70*
f	x	g	f	n	z	k	d	j	p	*80*
n	l	m	v	l	x	l	s	g	c	*90*
n	y	x	j	s	b	j	x	k	y	*100*
d	t	g	c	t	h	z	f	m	g	*110*
r	h	w	p	v	l	r	g	p	v	*120*
d	g	m	s	d	w	k	t	h	b	*130*

Figure 4. An example of a piece of Fit Learning curriculum used to build fluency in phonics skills.

of thousands of pieces of curriculum. And guess what? Our learners enthusiastically engage with all of our materials! How is this possible? Because they are explicitly reinforced for doing so. Children do not learn because of their *interest* in how the curriculum looks. They learn because they have behaved in a specific way with respect to that curriculum, and more important, that behavior has been repeatedly followed by reinforcement.

MYTH #6: IT'S ALL ABOUT SELF-ESTEEM

One goal that arose from those educational reform efforts in the early 20th century was the development of self-esteem.[35] The progressive ideology values self-esteem above all other educational goals and views the achievement of self-esteem as separate and somewhat contradictory to the achievement of academic competence.[8] It is widely believed that pushing students to achieve academic competence can actually damage self-esteem. So the myth that the primary goal of education is to encourage self-esteem was born.

Clearly, we want students to feel confident in themselves. Unfortunately, the progressive rhetoric regarding this value often does not translate into reality. Self-esteem has served as a notorious scapegoat for the systemic failures by schools to effectively educate the majority of students. Year after year, schools excuse abysmal test scores by declaring they emphasize development of the whole child by prioritizing self-esteem over academic achievement.[8] Large-scale studies have identified teaching practices based in behavioral science to vastly improve academic achievement as well as self-esteem. However, the establishment has consistently denied such findings by falsely suggesting that such methods ignore self-esteem. Self-esteem has become a slippery slope, which the establishment uses to justify the continued use of ineffective practices and the failure to produce academic proficiency with a majority of students.

Self-esteem is a *construct* that is difficult to define and measure. Again, behavior serves as the only evidence available—in other words, individuals engage in behaviors that serve as evidence of high or low self-esteem. My organization continuously produces learners who are described as confident, perseverant, fearless, successful, independent, and vital. In short, we produce high self-esteem with our learners. However, we define self-esteem in more objective, behavioral terms. For example, we might count the number of positive statements made throughout a session, the number of times a learner agrees to practice a difficult skill again, or the number of times a learner attempts new, more difficult tasks. These are all behavioral measures of what society at large might describe as evidence of high self-esteem.

It is the achievement of academic competence that leads to increases in the behaviors society at large would call evidence of high self-esteem. However, we don't achieve these improvements by targeting self-esteem. We achieve them by producing fluency in academic skills. Other large-scale studies, which the establishment has repeatedly tried to refute, support these same findings, which I will describe in detail in Chapter 7.[8] Education is about academic achievement, and it is academic achievement that leads learners to value hard work, persevere through failure, and willingly tackle new, more difficult challenges. Academic competence produces high self-esteem, not the other way around.

MYTH #7: BUT THEY'RE THE EXPERTS

Throughout my career, I have spoken with countless parents who express complete shock when I tell them that what they have been told about the causes for their child's skills deficits or problem behavior is most likely *wrong*. Their first reaction is to say, "But the people who have said these things to me are the experts, aren't they?" And herein lies our problem. Let's take on these "experts" one by one.

Expert 1: The Teacher

Parents are usually first alerted to the fact that their child is struggling academically by their child's teacher. I spent a good deal of time in this book describing the tragic inadequacies of teacher-training programs. The establishment actually trains teachers away from the intentional design of learning environments to promote learning and mastery. Teachers are told that children learn via development and exposure to experiences. They are trained to believe that children should construct their own realities and explore their worlds. Directly teaching skills or, god forbid, providing drill and practice opportunities is largely forbidden by the educational establishment. Again, none of these notions are based on the empirically validated principles of learning. All stem from the beliefs of the educational establishment.

So when learners fail, the only option teachers have is to assume something is *wrong* with them. When academic failure becomes significantly problematic, it is a teacher who usually recommends that a child be evaluated for a learning disability. Most parents blindly follow this recommendation and schedule an evaluation of their child, which is typically performed by a school psychologist or a private neuropsychologist. So a member of the psychological establishment is usually next on the scene.

Expert 2: The Neuropsychologist

Psychologists are trained in different methods than those guided by natural science. The psychological establishment adheres to deductive rather than inductive methods. Deductive practices involve coming up with a theory and then collecting evidence to prove or disprove the theory. As mentioned previously, natural science is not about theory-proving. Natural science is about making direct observations of a phenomenon as it is occurring over time so that causal relations are discovered. Theory-proving, a very different practice, involves making observations and then making inferences about those observations based on a theory. In other words, the important part of the work is the *inferences* made about what was observed rather than the observations themselves.

Psychologists use these deductive methods in their evaluations of learners. In psychological testing, a learner's performance is measured with a variety of assessments. Based on that performance, the psychologist makes inferences about why the learner performed in that way. The performance is seen as evidence of inherent characteristics of the learner like intelligence, aptitude, or neurological dysfunction. Again, as I have said before, the psychologist cannot make direct observations of these inherent characteristics. These are inferences made about the behavior observed. These inferences are presented to parents as facts, where the learner is said to *have* low IQ, low aptitude, inherent neurological dysfunction, or a learning disability. However, the only fact is how the learner behaved with respect to an assessment. Everything the psychologist says about the reason for that performance is inferred and, fundamentally, not real.

From a psychological evaluation, two things typically happen. First, a child is diagnosed, or labeled, with a learning disability. Second, the psychologist makes recommendations. These recommendations sometimes include medication, as in the case of a diagnosis of Attention Deficit Disorder (ADD). I will get to the medication nightmare in a moment. But first, these recommendations always include classroom or school-based *accommodations*. In other words, since the learner has been identified as having a supposed disability, the only option involves helping the child *cope* with this disability. Accommodations typically include things like seating in the front of the classroom, longer time on tests, modified assignments, and special education services provided by the school. Just as a reminder, over 90% of learners classified as LD graduate below proficiency in all academic subjects. Our NAEP results clearly indicate the tragic ineffectiveness of these kinds of accommodations and services.

There are other problems with psychologists making recommendations of this sort. First and foremost, psychologists who diagnose children with learning disabilities have not evaluated *learning* at all. Testing a child once is a measure of performance. Performance and learning are very different things. As I have said, learning is the change in behavior over time. We can understand nothing about learning by measuring a learner's behavior once. We can only understand learning by observing behavior and measuring it over time as it occurs in the learning environment. Psychologists who conduct testing are *not* experts in learning. They are most certainly not experts in how to accelerate learning or correct skills deficits, and this fact is abundantly clear by their recommendations, which often serve only to handicap children further and ensure that their skills deficits become a life sentence, as the proficiency rates of children classified as learning disabled indicate.

Expert 3: The Pediatrician

Based on an inferred diagnosis of ADD, psychologists will often recommend medication. Thus, a child's primary care physician is usually next on the scene. However, primary care physicians may become involved earlier on in this process and may make the initial referral for a child in their care to be evaluated for a learning disability. Regardless of how it occurs, a member of the medical establishment can become involved in academic issues or concerns regarding problem behavior.

Although physicians are highly trained in their subject matter, they are not trained in behavioral science. Due to the tendency to confuse behavioral issues with medical ones, issues around learning and behavior can seem to be within a medical doctor's expertise. Thus doctors are considered to be experts in areas where they are not. Luckily, some doctors understand this and make appropriate referrals. Unfortunately, many do not and take it upon themselves to either diagnose children with ADD during an office visit or refer them for neuropsychological evaluations.

Doctors are trained to infer disease based on observed symptoms. They are also trained to conduct tests or procedures whenever possible to verify their inferences. This model is appropriate for medical issues. However, this model is absolutely inappropriate for issues relating to learning and behavior. Because of this misunderstanding, learning deficits and behavioral problems established as a result of a learner's behavioral history are often medicalized and, worse, treated with medication.

MYTH #8: LEARNING AND BEHAVIORAL PROBLEMS ARE MEDICAL AND OFTEN REQUIRE MEDICATION

Evidence does exist that stimulant medications can be effective.[20] However, there is no evidence that these medications actually *treat* a medical condition at all—that is, lead to its cure and an end for a need for medication. Stimulant medications can improve certain types of behaviors associated with ADD but, for the improvements to be maintained, the child has to keep taking the medication. However, evidence also exists that behaviors associated with ADD can be improved with behavioral intervention without the kinds of side effects associated with stimulant medications.[106, 107]

Stimulant medications are performance-enhancing drugs.[20] Everyone benefits from stimulants to some degree, as evidenced by our civilization's dependence on caffeine. Stimulants wake us up. It is true that some children have neurological profiles that greatly benefit from stimulants. However, these children are the very rare exception. The occurrence of neurologically based ADD represents less than 1% of children, yet the current rate of children diagnosed with ADD is closer to 10% of the population: ten times more than it should be.[20]

The overdiagnosing, and thus overmedicating, of so many children is the tragic result of the establishments presenting themselves as experts in the area of learning and behavior. A majority of children with ADD diagnoses have behavioral issues that are the result of a history of reinforcement for maladaptive behaviors. These behaviors were not caused by ADD. ADD is a label, not an explanation. The actual cause for these behaviors lies in the history of their reinforcement. Effective treatment requires that the problem behavior no longer be reinforced, and that an alternative, adaptive behavior be practiced and reinforced instead. However, behavioral intervention requires patience and a long-term perspective. As I said before, we want to snap our fingers and have our children's behavior magically change. The idea that a child can take a pill that will fix their behavior or learning problems is quite appealing to the public. Unfortunately, as I hope I have clarified, learning doesn't work this way.

Many children diagnosed with ADD have significant academic deficits caused by ineffective instruction. Because they cannot successfully engage in the classroom, it should come as no surprise that these kids have difficulty paying attention. None of us would be able to sustain attention during an eight-hour lecture presented in Chinese if we do not speak the language, right? Yet we expect children to do this all day, every day—and to make matters worse, they get diagnosed with some pathology when they fail.

The bottom line is, even if medication has some kind of beneficial effect, the child still needs to acquire the skills that led to the diagnosis of ADD in the first place. Kids do not start magically reading, doing math, writing, or anything else as a result of taking medication. Medication may make children easier to instruct, but they still require effective instruction. If the same poorly designed teaching practices are used, children might be less disruptive in the classroom while still failing to master skills.

Another tragic practice in the medication of children is the lack of evidence involved. Behavioral scientists would never begin an intervention with a child without taking measures of the behavior before, during, and after its implementation. Behavioral scientists practice natural science. In this sense, we continuously measure behavior and systematically analyze the effectiveness of our interventions. If our data indicate that an intervention is not effective, we discontinue it and try something else. Few medical doctors do this with respect to introducing medication as a behavioral intervention. This practice is profoundly unethical.

The only means of objectively determining whether a behavioral intervention is effective is to measure its effects over time. However, doctors typically diagnose a child with ADD during an office visit based on a questionnaire given to a caregiver. Medication is then prescribed to treat the behavioral issues described by the caregiver—case closed. Objective measures of the supposed behavioral issue are not made before the medication is prescribed to verify whether such behaviors are actually occurring or to determine their severity. Similarly, objective measures of behavior following the introduction of a medication are not taken after it is administered to determine its effectiveness. The process relies on a caregiver's word that there is a problem in the first place, and determining the medication's effectiveness based on the caregiver's opinion. This process is in *no way* scientific and has led to the rampant overuse of medications with harmful side effects.

In my 20-year career, less than 1% of our learners have had real, neurological learning impairments. The remainder were academically failed by ineffective teaching practices, yet many of their parents had been told that these failures were due to some inherent disability. These so-called experts were wrong. Naming a skills deficit or behavioral problem is not explaining it and does not lead to the design of effective interventions. If you have to invent mythical causes to explain behavior, then you are most certainly not an expert.

MYTH #9: IT'S ALL ABOUT THE BRAIN

As I previously mentioned, we are absolutely brain-obsessed as a culture. Viewing the brain as the cause of everything we do and learn fits into our beliefs regarding the metaphysical nature of our existence. If we must acknowledge that there are forces controlling our behavior, it's best that those forces reside inside of us; otherwise our freedom and dignity are seemingly threatened.[92] In this way, the psychological establishment reflects the beliefs of the greater culture and also preserves the idea of human beings ultimately being free and in charge of their own actions. The psychological establishment has worked quite hard to legitimize the notion of an inner controlling agent by localizing that control to the brain. This brings us to the final myth about learning, otherwise known as "It's all about the brain."

Due to misrepresentations by the psychological establishment, the public believes that our brains control everything we do. When learners struggle academically, it is immediately assumed that there is something wrong with their brains. Countless parents say to me that the reason their children struggle in reading, math, or some other academic area is because their brains just aren't *wired* for those things. The public fundamentally believes that we are born with our brains hardwired in particular ways and that children develop over time largely due to these "microprocessors" they are born with. However, nothing could be further from the case!

First of all, brains are not computers. Computers are notoriously used as metaphors for the brain, but these metaphors are pretty dangerous. Computers are machines invented by humans. Brains are not. Brains are profoundly complex organs within an entire system of organs and processes that make us human. The brain is one part of this complex system. This system does not work without the brain and the brain does not work without the system. We cannot separate one from the other. Just because the psychological establishment wants to ideologically elevate the brain above all else does not make it true. Brain dominance is a *theory*. The brain doesn't change without behavior and behavior doesn't change without the brain. When a person behaves, the *entire* person does so, not just one part of it. To understand behavior requires an analysis of the *entire* person behaving with respect to their historical and current context, which is the subject matter of behavioral science.

Recent discoveries in neuroscience support my assertion of the symbiotic relationship between brain and behavior.[25, 74–81] As we behave, and that behavior comes into contact with some consequence in the environment, neural processes simultaneously occur. The symbiotic relationship between brain and behavior actually makes sense from an evolutionary perspective. We have evolved as a species with brains that are capable of *responding and adapting* to our own unique environments. In other words, we have evolved as a species with the ability to learn from our individual experiences. The assumption that learning is *dictated or controlled* by the brain is largely false. Learning results from the brain responding and adapting as the entire person behaves in their environment.

Learning occurs when we repeatedly behave in a specific way and, most important, this behavior is repeatedly reinforced. This process ultimately results in the behavior increasing in strength—measured as rate of response—until it reaches a level synonymous with neurological permanence. As behavioral scientists, we don't measure these neurological changes because we don't have access to those. Rather, we measure *behavioral* changes. However, a reliable assumption can be made that if behavior is changing, then neurology is also changing. In other words, the entire person is changing. We need not stick electrodes on learners' brains to measure learning because B. F. Skinner gave us *rate of response* and Ogden Lindsley gave us *celeration*: behavioral measures that provide us all of the information we need to determine if learning is taking place. What amazing contributions to the world!

When kids fail to learn something, this failure likely has nothing to do with a brain problem. Learning is largely determined by our interactions in the environment, so when a learner fails, we should first look to their environment. Remember our infant in the crib? Sometimes all we need to do is metaphorically lower the mobile, make some small environmental adjustment and, boom, learning occurs. If a child has not effectively mastered a skill, I promise they also do not have the neurology that corresponds with being masterful at that skill. They don't have this neurology because it is produced by the act of learning itself. That neurology doesn't exist ahead of time, dictating and driving kids to learn things. That neurology is actually a *result* of learning, and in order for it to be established, the learner must repeatedly behave in the desired way and that behavior must be repeatedly reinforced over time.

There are real neurological impairments that impact learning, and none of what I have said should be interpreted as a denial of such impairments. Traumatic brain injury is real. Autism is real. Down Syndrome is real. In rare cases, ADD is real. However, even kids with these kinds of disabilities can effectively learn from their environments. Ultimately, what they can learn and how quickly they can learn it may be quite different from those without their neurological profiles, but these children can learn from their environments just like everyone else. Their environments require the kind of precise design afforded only by the scientific understanding of human behavior offered by behavioral science, which is why our science leads to the design of the most effective interventions for individuals with disabilities. In fact, the application of our science to the treatment of autism and related disorders has been empirically validated as the *most* effective treatment for such disorders.[108-111]

Unfortunately, a tragic state of affairs occurs when a child's disability becomes the scapegoat for everything. Why does Johnny scream and tantrum? He has autism. Why can't Julie read? She has Down

Syndrome. Why can't Stevie finish his assignments? He has ADD. Again, even if the child's disability is real, that disability does not then also explain all of their behavioral deficits and excesses. Children with disabilities acquire maladaptive behavior in the same way as every-one else, by repeatedly behaving this way and having this behavior reinforced. Their disability may increase the likelihood that problem behavior occurs in the first place, but it becomes established as a part of that child's repertoire through a history of reinforcement for that behavior, just as it does for a child without a disability. Similarly, when children with disabilities fail to acquire adaptive skills, their disability does not also explain this failure. The failure to acquire skills results from ineffective instruction, just like for children without disabilities. All children require effective instruction if they are to master skills, including children with real disabilities.

The take-home point here is that the myths that dominate education, and our culture more generally, do not lead to *effective action*. These myths provide excuses for persistent academic failure, which occurs because the traditions followed by the establishments fundamentally do not work. In contrast, behavioral science has led us to understand how to design profoundly effective teaching practices that work for all learners. Instruction based in behavioral science defines our Technol-ogy of Teaching, which has the potential to empower our nation's youth and save them all from lifetimes of mediocrity and failure.

6

THE SOLUTION

"*The learner knows best.*"
—OGDEN LINDSLEY[112]

As our behavior occurs and comes into contact with reinforcing consequences in our environment, it increases in rate—becomes faster—until it is established as a permanent part of our repertoire. In other words, with enough repeated reinforcement over time, behavior becomes *habitual.*

Habitual behavior persists over time, occurs frequently, and appears automatic or effortless. Most people think of habits as undesirable behaviors that are difficult to get rid of, like biting our fingernails. But the term "habit" refers to any persistent behavior that occurs at a high rate—desirable or undesirable. Throwing tantrums, whining, word-guessing, reading, or computing math problems are all behaviors—things we *do*—and they can all become habits if frequently followed by reinforcement over time.

The Technology of Teaching designs instruction so that academic skills become habitual or established as effective habits. We prefer to use the term *fluent* to refer to academic habits.[105, 113–115] Fluent skills are rapid, automatic, and effortless. Fluent skills are remembered, easily usable for learning more complex things, and resistant to distractions or fatigue. Fluent skills are truly *mastered*. Thus, a truly mastered skill is a habit—a persistent skill a child can easily and readily engage in wherever and whenever they need to.

As we have seen, educational practices in this country do not produce effective academic habits. Due to inadequate training, teachers don't design instruction in a way that produces fluent repertoires and, more often than not, students end up acquiring ineffective habits, like Alex's word-guessing. Teachers must follow rules and timelines set by the establishment rather than being allowed to act as scientists and adjust instruction to the individual performance of their students. Unfortunately, as I hope you now realize, children don't learn according to arbitrary timelines.

Behavioral science has led to the discovery that learning occurs, and only occurs, through its repeated reinforcement over time. Thus, effective instruction requires that learners engage in repeated, reinforced practice of skills until they are fluent. The time required to achieve fluency varies across learners and skills. The learning process may fundamentally be the same, but the time required for that process to occur is highly individualized. Moreover, complex repertoires must be shaped over time through the repeated, reinforced practice of essential component skills. Students cannot engage in more complex repertoires until the component skills included in that complex repertoire are mastered.

My organization uses behavioral science and the Technology of Teaching for the production of fluent academic repertoires with every type of student. For more than 20 years, we have made vast discoveries about how children learn and truly master academic skills. We made these discoveries by conducting applied, natural science with each individual learner. We didn't make these discoveries by working with groups of students. We made these discoveries by working with students individually, so that we understand learning at the level of *process*.

By understanding learning as a process, I mean the analysis of each learner's individual Standard Celeration Charts (SCCs) generated for each skill targeted throughout the course of training. As in the example of the infant in the crib, it is the analysis of learning through the use of the SCC that allows us to evaluate the impact of specific instructional variables on the learning of each student over time. In this sense, we gain a profound understanding of what specific features of the learning environment accelerate or interfere with learning at the level of the individual student. We systematically replicate these findings across learners and skills to identify generalities or *principles* of instruction. More often than not, these instructional principles are effective with most learners. However, there are nuances to specific learners that require further modification of those general instructional principles to ensure maximum learning gains. It is only through this kind of process-level analysis that we are able to design effective instruction for every single learner. It is the practice of natural science in our applied setting that gives us access to understanding learning at the level of process.

Our process-level analysis occurs as the act of instruction itself. We conduct one-on-one sessions where each learner is individually paired with a certified learning coach. During sessions, we implement effective instruction, conduct practice timings, immediately deliver reinforcement or corrective feedback on performance, collect data on the rate of each skill performed, chart those data on individual SCCs for every skill, adjust variables related to instruction in a systematic manner to accelerate learning, and evaluate the manipulation of those variables over time to ensure that learning and mastery occurs. In this way, each of our Fit Learning locations functions as a learning laboratory, contributing to a collective knowledge base regarding how to most rapidly accelerate learning gains with students.

Critics of our approach claim what we do works simply because we are able to work one-on-one with students. Although working with an individual student naturally has many advantages over working with groups of students, the effectiveness of our approach cannot be accounted for simply by the fact that it's one-on-one. Most "tutoring" operates this way, yet no traditional tutoring approach comes close to producing more than a year's growth in as little as 40 hours, which, as I have said, is the outcome we have been producing for over 20 years.

Moreover, many of the school-based special education services that students classified as LD receive are also one-on-one. I have already shared the tragic inadequacies of services like these, indicated by the fact that more than 90% of students classified as LD graduate below proficiency.[1] Our approach doesn't work because it's one-on-one. Our approach works because of behavioral science and the Technology of Teaching.

The establishments also claim that the Technology of Teaching could never be effectively implemented in a classroom with groups of students. However, the methods we use were originally developed for classrooms and large-scale studies have indicated their effectiveness with groups of students. I will share that evidence with you in the following chapter.

Natural science always begins at the individual level. The phenomenon of interest must first be studied over time at the level of the individual. As the scientific method leads to the discovery of causal relations and is systematically replicated over time, generalities or laws are discovered. It is only after these general principles are discovered and replicated at the individual level that they can then be tested at the group level. At Fit Learning, we conduct the essential process-level science that, for many reasons, schools can't possibly conduct. We are contributing to a collective knowledge base about effective instructional practices that schools can then benefit from by testing these practices in the classroom. Scientific discoveries always happen this way.

THE TECHNOLOGY OF TEACHING

Our Technology of Teaching entails three major methods: Precision Teaching, Direct Instruction, and Curriculum-Based Measurement. Behavioral science serves as the underlying framework for everything we do; however, there are three major methods integrated into what we call the Technology of Teaching, which I'll describe. I will conclude with recommendations for how the Technology of Teaching can be effectively implemented in our nation's schools.

Precision Teaching

Precision Teaching (PT) refers to the use of the Standard Celeration Chart (SCC) for the analysis of learning and instruction.[9, 112, 113, 116–124] Ogden Lindsley, whom I previously introduced to you as the developer of the SCC, is also the founder of PT, and he designed this chart specifically for teachers. He wanted to put into the hands of teachers the same precise, analytic tool used by behavioral scientists in the laboratory setting. In other words, Lindsley created PT so that teachers could function as scientists.

As I demonstrated with our infant in the crib example, the SCC enables the precise evaluation of learning over time and allows teachers to immediately determine the effectiveness of their instruction. At Fit Learning, we use the SCC to evaluate every single skill targeted with every single learner. However, before we determine what skills we need to target, we must first determine where we need to start.

Comprehensive Skills Assessments

The first step in our process entails assessing a learner so that core skill levels can be *precisely* identified, as we did with Alex. We have discovered the essential component skills children must master and how to determine when mastery has truly been achieved. We do not account for their current academic deficits as the product of some inherent disorder, even if an actual neurological impairment exists. Rather, we account for their current deficits in terms of their individual learning histories.

For example, as I described for Alex, learners who present as poor readers are evaluated in terms of their ability to employ essential tool skills for reading such as identifying phonics sounds, discriminating between vowels and consonants, identifying phonetic rules (e.g., short versus long vowel words), decoding words according to these phonetic rules, and so forth. Similarly, learners struggling in math are evaluated in terms of basic numeracy and computation skills like skip counting, identifying numbers, using place value, and performing basic addition, subtraction, multiplication, and division. We have developed comprehensive core skills assessments for every major academic domain: reading, spelling, comprehension, mathematics, logical problem-solving, grammar, and expressive writing. We even have core skills assessments for penmanship and "learning to learn" skills for very young learners. In this way, we can understand learners' current academic deficits in terms of their individual learning histories and, specifically, their failure to properly master essential component skills.

Each of these tool skills is measured in separate, timed assessment periods in order to identify rates of those skills. As previously explained, rate serves as the fundamental measure of behavior. Rate gives us a precise measure of the behavior and allows us to make reliable predictions about its strength or the probability that the behavior will continue to occur. Due to our adherence to rate as a measure of behavior, we have discovered what mastery of skills actually means and how it can be measured. We have discovered that high rates of correct responding over time predict that a skill is neurologically permanent (i.e., remembered or retained), usable for learning more complex things, and resistant to distractions and fatigue.[12, 105, 113–115] In other words, fast, accurate, effortless performance is what determines if a skill is truly mastered. As I have said, we call this type of mastery fluency. Fluency is commonly used in the vernacular to refer to skills that are seemingly second nature: effortless, fluid, automatic, or indicative of expertise. Unfortunately, fluency is most often associated with inherent talent. I have already addressed the unfortunate result of viewing talent as a causal factor. But fluency is a *measurable* type of performance intentionally produced through the repeated, reinforced practice of skills.

Notice that our measure of mastery does not entail letter grades, a numbering system, happy faces, or subjective reports regarding student performance. Our measure of mastery does not even entail percent correct — the most common measure used in education. None of the measures or grading practices used in education are scientifically valid measures of learning or performance. As for percent correct, accuracy alone does not indicate that a skill has been truly mastered.

The Problem with Percent Correct

Imagine two learners, Sally and Susan, completing a 50-problem math test. Sally completes the math test in 10 minutes, but Susan requires an entire hour to complete it. Nevertheless, they both score 100%. Since they both received perfect scores, there is nothing more to worry about, right? Wrong. If we analyze their performance in terms of rate rather than percent correct, we see a very different learning picture. Sally completed the test at a rate of five problems per minute and Susan completed the test at a rate of less than one problem per minute. In other words, Sally is five times faster (or more fluent) than Susan. Neither made errors, but Susan required five times longer to accomplish this score than Sally. So Susan could benefit from more practice on these types of math problems in order for this skill to be truly mastered.

When time is excluded from the measurement of learning, important aspects of learning and mastery go undetected. Neurological permanence is not produced by correctness. It is produced by the repeated, reinforced practice of a skill until it is fluent. You cannot measure fluency with percent correct or other common measures found in education. You can *only* measure fluency as rate or count per time.

Fluency Aims and Functional Mastery

Fit Learning, and PT more generally, has identified the levels of fluency learners must achieve for true mastery of thousands of skills. These levels are known as *fluency aims*.[125] Fluency aims are initially identified by testing the experts in a skill. In other words, we measure the rate of that skill being performed by an expert. This sets the initial aim for a skill or the rate we are *aiming* for throughout the course of training. For example, our fluency aim for math facts is 50 correct answers per minute; our fluency aim for phonics is 100 letter sounds per minute; our fluency aim for sounding out words is 120 sounds and words per minute, and so forth.

However, we also test for fluency with every single learner throughout the course of training to determine if mastery has actually been achieved. Specifically, we check the skill after extended periods of time without practice to ensure that it is remembered and remains fluent even in the absence of ongoing practice. We test the skill for longer and longer time periods and in the face of distracting conditions to ensure that it remains fluent. Finally, we continually test more complex skills to evaluate if the skill we are training to fluency is leading to the improved performance of something more difficult. Our fluency aims serve as a guide, but mastery is determined on an individual basis for every single learner.

In this sense, we approach mastery *functionally*, meaning that we systematically evaluate the impact a learner's performance makes on other types of performance. Rather than being meaningless and arbitrary, our mastery criteria actually mean something for the learner and, more important, predict very important characteristics of future performance. Our fluency aims are designed to produce the kinds of outcomes that are of profound value to learners: the retention of skills over time in the absence of practice, the ability to perform skills for lengthy testing periods or in distracting or suboptimal conditions, and the ability to apply skills for the learning of more complex skills.[12] These characteristics serve as our goals for instruction with every learner.

Variation Is the Nature of Human Learning

Over the course of my career, no learner I have seen has followed the same path to fluency. Learners master some skills quite quickly and can effectively leap ahead in a curriculum sequence; however, other skills take more time to master and often require teaching strategies to be modified for fluency to be achieved. Not only is there variation in how learning goes across skills for a single learner, there is significant variation in how learning goes across learners.

The fact that learners do not learn at the same pace is not indicative of a pathology or problem. Variation is the fundamental nature of human learning. Children do not learn as a group; they learn as individuals. Even though, due to necessity, we must educate children in groups, this does not also mean that they learn as a group. They most certainly do not, and the evidence is clear from our nation's abysmal NAEP scores. If we must instruct children in groups, we had better employ practices that allow us to design instruction for each individual learner or our educational system will never improve. PT is the practice of individualizing instruction for the benefit of all learners.

Behavior Multiplies, So We Go for "Times Twos"

I have defined learning as the change in behavior over time. I previously explained that we measure learning in this way through celeration—acceleration of skills we are trying to increase and deceleration of behaviors we are trying to decrease or get rid of. I have also explained that we use the term celeration because behavior changes by multiplying and dividing, not adding or subtracting. In other words, with effective teaching practices, we can increase learning *exponentially*. It is through celeration that the real variations in learning become clear. It is also through celeration that we can determine how rapidly learning is occurring.

Fit Learning adheres to a standard of producing a minimum of *times two* accelerations on skills. What does that mean in lay terms? It means that, at a minimum, we are doubling a learner's performance each week. For example, an increase of 10 correct math facts per minute at the beginning of the week to 20 correct math facts per minute at the end of the week. An increase from 10 to 20 is a *times two* increase. If we aren't producing times two or better weekly celerations, then learning isn't happening fast enough, and we must change our teaching practice in some way to accelerate it. Fit Learning, and PT more generally, has repeatedly demonstrated that times two or greater weekly learning gains are highly significant. When learners achieve times twos, they become aware of their own success and the people in their lives notice it too.

The Learner Knows Best

Once the levels of essential component skills have been identified for a learner, a fluency-building program can be designed to move deficient skills to mastery. Learners must master first things first before they can effectively learn and perform more complex skills. Sadly, educators are actually trained to believe the opposite. They are taught that learners move through a sequence of skills based on the passage of time or the subjective judgement of a teacher, not as a result of true mastery of each prerequisite step.

However, it is the learner who should determine when they move ahead in a curriculum sequence. In this sense, *the learner knows best*: a favorite mantra of our friend Ogden Lindsley.[112] This means that it is the learner's performance in its ongoing measurement over time that tells us when mastery has been achieved, and thus, when the learner is ready to move up the curriculum ladder to learn something more difficult. The *learner knows best* mantra does not imply that the learner's opinion guides movement through a curriculum sequence, just as that movement should not be based on the opinion of the teacher. Rather, the ongoing measurement of that learner's behavior informs the educator when advancement should occur.

Agility and Cognitive Fitness

PT has repeatedly demonstrated that when learners achieve fluency on basic skills, they begin leaping up curriculum ladders effortlessly and engaging in more complex skills with little training required, a phenomenon known as *agility*.[10] At Fit Learning, we also refer to it as *cognitive fitness*. In other words, the more fluent learners become, the better they get at learning in general. Our measurement system (i.e., the Standard Celeration Chart or SCC), gives us an ongoing historical record of learning across skills. Through this record, we have discovered that learners begin achieving fluency on new skills more quickly as a function of their achieving fluency on prerequisite skills. We have also discovered that accuracy improves more quickly, learners show less variability in performance on new skills, and learners begin engaging in the performance of more complex skills with little to no training required. In other words, we start getting free stuff from our learners. Everyone likes free stuff, right?

Education should involve being as efficient as possible. We should be using teaching strategies that produce *generative* gains — gains that are not produced by direct training but are a collateral benefit of the direct training in other areas.[11, 99, 100, 126] We have a lot of children to educate and very little time to accomplish such a daunting task. If history has taught us anything, it is that determining what is most effective and most efficient requires science, not guessing, opinions, beliefs, subjective interpretations, or the like. Prescientific practices have never led to the discovery of what is effective or efficient. It is science that leads us to such discoveries, and it is science that led us to make those same discoveries regarding human learning. Now we must implement these scientific practices in the classroom.

Practice Makes Perfect . . . If It's Perfect Practice

The achievement of fluency, or true mastery, requires "deliberate, purposeful" practice.[25] In other words, not all practice is created equal, and poorly designed practice can actually be detrimental to learning and mastery. Fit Learning, and PT in general, has perfected the design of this type of practice. First and foremost, all practice should involve the precise measurement of the skill being practiced. Because rate is the fundamental measure of behavior and celeration is the fundamental measure of learning, rate should be measured during practice. Rate during daily practice should be plotted over time using the SCC so that celerations can be generated and the effectiveness of this practice reliably evaluated and improved when necessary.

Rate entails time, so practice should occur during timed periods, which we call practice *timings*. Practice timings can be as short as 15 seconds or as long as five minutes, depending on the skill being trained and the profile of the learner. More often than not, practice should begin with short timings (e.g., 15 seconds), which we call *sprints*.[113] When a learner first embarks on mastering a skill, it can feel very difficult. Try writing the alphabet with your nondominant hand or counting backward from 2,000 by multiples of 13 and you will get an idea of how learners feel during the initial stages of practice. It is important to start with short timings and gradually shape the timing length to longer and longer periods as the learner achieves fluency during shorter periods.

The Personal Best

Practicing to fluency is not easy. Think of increasing the speed in which you run a mile or increasing the number of miles you run each time. Reaching such goals is hard work. Of course, there are individuals who are personally motivated to achieve such goals. More often than not, however, learners are not motivated to put forth the kind of effort required to truly master skills. Due to their failed learning histories, most learners attempt to escape or avoid difficult academic tasks. A skill that is not mastered, or is *dysfluent,* feels effortful, difficult, aversive, or unpleasant. In short, learners tend to avoid dysfluent skills at all costs.

Going back to our propensity to invent mythical causes for behavior, a learner's avoidance of academic tasks tends to be explained in terms of inherent laziness, anxiety, lack of motivation, low self-determination, or a poor work ethic. But none of these actually *explain* the learner's avoidance and certainly do not lead to effective actions to change the learner's behavior. More often than not, the only option is further punishment of the learner, who is already a victim of punishing consequences. It is this history of punitive consequences along with long-term academic failure as a result of ineffective teaching practices that actually explains the learner's behavior. It is only by changing the consequences and teaching practices that effective action becomes possible.

This notion brings us back to the principle of shaping previously described. We cannot expect an unmotivated learner with deficient skills to magically begin performing skills because we expect, or worse, demand it. This notion is absurd, unethical, and, as our NAEP scores indicate, profoundly ineffective. We must begin shaping first things first in timed, practice periods where the increasing rate of the skill being trained can be precisely measured to determine the effectiveness of the practice opportunities we have designed. This kind of shaping is best accomplished through reinforcement of the Personal Best, or PBs as we call them at Fit Learning.

Rather than expecting a learner to achieve fluency immediately when practice begins, we set Personal Best goals for each learner on each skill where reinforcement is delivered for small, manageable increases in performance over time until mastery is ultimately achieved. For example, if a learner achieved 20 correct math facts per minute during the previous practice session, then their first PB of the day would be the achievement of 21 correct math facts per minute. When a PB is achieved, some type of reinforcer is immediately delivered. For some learners, enthusiastic praise and high fives is all it takes. Others may require points exchangeable for prizes or privileges of some sort. What functions as a reinforcer varies with the individual and must be identified on an individual basis. Learners with longer histories of failure require more powerful motivational systems than others. Regardless, with the right reinforcer and the careful shaping of skills through the achievement of Personal Bests, *any* learner can achieve fluency—or true mastery—of essential academic skills and look forward to a future of academic and personal success.

Everybody Needs a Coach

Even with shaping and the systematic reinforcement of Personal Best goals, achieving fluency is hard work. Completing a math worksheet of 50 problems in an entire class period is not the same as completing 50 math facts per minute, which is our fluency aim for basic computation. This type of performance requires intense focus, concentration, and perseverance, which are natural byproducts of fluency-based practice. With PT, students learn to persevere through challenging experiences; an essential life skill that, unfortunately, many children never acquire. Even with the Personal Best goal, learners are not necessarily going to achieve it on the first, second, or even third attempt. They are going to have to repeatedly try again to achieve their goals. This can produce some discomfort, frustration, and a tendency to quit, which brings us to the importance of having a coach.[25]

The remarkable individuals formally certified to work at Fit Learning are called *learning coaches*. A coach is someone who encourages you to do things you may not initially want to do so that you can ultimately achieve all that you want to achieve. A coach provides the kind of encouragement and feedback required to work through challenges that are difficult. A coach never lets us quit. Just as athletes require coaches, learners do too. Everybody needs a coach. Teachers should function as coaches and there should be multiple coaches in the classroom trained in the kinds of motivational strategies that work to push students through challenging moments in learning so they can discover their own greatness and eventually learn how to push themselves.

The Myth of Intrinsic Motivation

The discussion of learning to push through challenging moments brings us to the issue of *intrinsic motivation*. The notion that some people are born motivated and others are not is one of the more damaging myths out there.[127] What we call intrinsic motivation is actually learned. Like other hypothetical constructs, intrinsic motivation is simply a label used to characterize certain patterns of behavior. People who are called intrinsically motivated appear to work hard without obvious payoffs, or reinforcers, for that behavior. However, those reinforcers are occurring; they are just not detectable to the layperson. Engaging in the behavior itself has most likely become the reinforcer.

When behavior becomes fluent, it is something we want to do. We all prefer to do the things we are good at. However, to get good at something requires that we practice it repeatedly over time. During the stage of getting good at something, other kinds of reinforcers are required. Praise from a teacher, parent, or peer; access to free-time activities; or grades or awards are all examples of the kinds of external reinforcers that initially follow the practice of skills during the early stages of learning. If we are lucky, these external reinforcers work to strengthen and establish the skill to such a degree that engagement in the skill alone provides reinforcement. Thus, it can appear that we are intrinsically motivated, self-determined, self-motivated, or have a strong work ethic. Again, it is easy to explain behavior by naming it. However, the true explanation for the behavior of hard-working individuals can be found in their learning histories. More often than not, such people had a really effective *coach* shaping and reinforcing their behavior along the way.

The Myth of Rote Learning

When we talk about practice, it somehow becomes synonymous with *rote learning*, which is a bad term to the educational establishment. This is another learning myth promulgated by the so-called experts. Rote learning typically refers to the process of memorization or the recalling of facts or information.[128] However, rote learning is not a principle of learning at all. It is a description of behavior that is confused with learning. Rote learning refers to a learner's behavior when they respond to academic subject matter in a specific, discrete, or finite way. In other words, when presented with $2 + 3 = ?$ the learner responds "5." Responding in this way is largely necessary in education. There is a vast amount of information that children just need to know, and they should practice responding to such material until they can do so fluently. However, children learning anything by *rote* has been given such a bad name in education that it is actively prevented in the classroom. Again, this notion is based on the ideas of the educational establishment, which assert that directly teaching skills or drilling facts damages creativity, critical thinking, and problem-solving—a completely ludicrous notion.

It is true that recalling facts is different from explaining, relating, integrating, or otherwise engaging with information. However, to suggest that recalling facts interferes with behaving in other ways with respect to that material is completely false. Children must know that $2 + 3 = 5$. Period. However, is knowing that $2 + 3 = 5$ enough to ensure that a learner can solve a more complex word problem that involves that same equation? Not necessarily. Knowing basic math facts is an *essential* component skill for solving more complex math operations like word problems. However, there are other skills required for solving more complex problems that children must also master in order to effectively solve such problems. But to suggest that learning $2 + 3 = 5$ actually interferes with a learner's ability to solve a complex word problem is completely absurd and empirically invalid. This misunderstanding stems from the erroneous view that complex problem-solving entails higher order cognitive processes, which are inherent characteristics of a learner that teachers simply foster through exposure to problem-solving activities.

Private Behavior

Problem-solving, critical thinking, inferencing, and other seemingly inaccessible activities are things learners *do* — behaviors learners engage in with respect to complex subject matter. Such skills require training, like any other skill. More important, these skills are typically part of a complex repertoire of behavior comprised of multiple component skills that all require training to mastery. Problem-solving is not a repertoire a learner can master all at once. Problem-solving entails many component skills in addition to fluency in math facts such as reading the problem, identifying the information provided, identifying the missing information, identifying unnecessary information, deriving the operation required to identify the missing information, and performing the operation to correctly solve the problem. If any one of these components is deficient, the entire problem-solving repertoire is impacted. Sadly, educators are not trained to view complex behavioral repertoires in this way, nor are they trained to break down complex repertoires into their component parts. So when learners struggle with complex repertoires of this sort, it is attributed to inherent characteristics of the learner, rather than to deficient component skills that can be strengthened through training.

Complex repertoires like thinking, comprehending or problem-solving are viewed by the establishments, and the culture at large, as mental activities that belong to the realm of metaphysical stuff. From this perspective, these activities are viewed as inherent aspects of human beings, like intelligence, that we are born with. The dominant view is that some students are good at these things and others are not. However, all of these seemingly "mental" activities are things people *do*. These are just things people do that are private: unobservable behaviors that occur inside the skin.

Talk Aloud Problem-Solving

Now, whenever a behavior is unobservable, it becomes a bit problematic with respect to natural science. When trying to effectively teach or change private behaviors, we must somehow make them public. In other words, we must get our students engaging in *overt* thinking, problem-solving, or comprehending. My organization uses Talk Aloud Problem-Solving (TAPS) when training these kinds of complex repertoires, which has extensive validation as a profoundly successful approach.[129] Our students are initially trained to *think out loud*. By requiring that they make their private behavior public, we are able to immediately identify errors in logic, skipped steps, or incorrectly identified steps so that we can provide immediate prompts, models, corrections, and reinforcers leading to the mastery of very complex repertoires. When the learner successfully masters a complex repertoire of this sort through TAPS, they can then successfully revert to engaging in these complex repertoires covertly. In other words, their public problem-solving becomes private once again and, because of the fluency initially established through TAPS, their covert repertoire occurs fluently as well.

Up to this point, we have addressed Precision Teaching, one aspect of our Technology of Teaching. Ultimately, PT is a measurement system based in natural science that enables educators to evaluate learning over time as a means of determining the effectiveness of their teaching practices and the achievement of true mastery of skills. It is also based on the principle that for learning to occur, skills must be repeatedly practiced and reinforced over time until their rate reaches a level of fluency indicative of neurological permanence, resistance to distractions and fatigue, and the effortless learning of more complex repertoires.

Ultimately, PT involves the analysis of instruction in relation to the *learner*. However, our Technology of Teaching also includes an analysis of *what* is being instructed. In other words, we must also analyze the presentation of curriculum or the material to be learned.

Direct Instruction

Our Technology of Teaching includes Direct Instruction (DI), which involves the logical analyses of curriculum sequences and the construction of *faultless communications* for the presentation of such curriculum sequences to learners.[13, 104, 130–132] Although it evolved separately from the field of behavioral science, the two naturally merged because the theoretical underpinnings of DI align with those of behavioral science.

First, DI uses inductive logic in the analyses of curriculum sequences where complex repertoires are analyzed into component parts for the instruction of first things first. Second, DI holds the educator and instructional environment accountable for learning—*not* the learner. The presentation of a concept is designed in such a way that miscommunications and errors in learning are minimized. Third, DI acknowledges the necessity of active participation by the learner during instruction along with the delivery of immediate, specific feedback regarding correct or incorrect responding. Fourth, DI presents concepts in accordance with the behavioral account of language whereby opportunities to frame concepts relationally are provided, leading to the rapid acquisition of the target concept by taking advantage of a child's established language repertoire. Finally, DI focuses on the production of generative repertoires where, from a small subset of examples, a concept is learned and then generatively applied to novel, untrained examples, thus increasing the efficiency of instruction.

Teaching Concepts with DI: An Example

Let's clarify what was offered above by using a concrete example. Let's consider teaching the concept of "square" to a young learner. The first tenet of DI entails using inductive logic to analyze the complex repertoire into its component parts. I know it seems strange to consider the concept of "square" as a complex repertoire but, to a naive learner, discriminating shapes is quite complex!

So we have a square, which when logically broken down can be identified as "a shape with four equal sides." Now, in this logical analysis of the components of the concept "square," we encounter four other components that our young learner must have preexisting knowledge of if our rule about the concept of squareness is going to be effective in teaching the discrimination. Our learner must know the concepts of "shape," "equal," "four," and "sides" if we are to use that rule to create a faultless communication. Hence, in this seemingly simple example, we see the extraordinary complexity involved in teaching even rudimentary concepts.

For the sake of solidifying the importance of faultless communications, let's assume that our imaginary learner does not have preexisting knowledge of "shape," "equal," "four," or "sides," yet we are still charged with the task of teaching the child the concept of "square." How can this instruction possibly occur? It can occur through the construction of a communication that capitalizes on the learner's preexisting language repertoire of relating stimuli according to sameness and difference, which we reviewed earlier. Constructing communications that occasion a learner's relational responding with respect to sameness and difference requires that we juxtapose positive and negative examples in a systematic manner. The way a teacher well trained in the principles of DI might approach the teaching of "square" is as follows:

TEACHER	CLASS RESPONDING IN UNISON
Draws a square on the board. Points to it. "This is a square. Say it."	"Square!"
"Perfect!" Draws a smaller square using a different color of marker. Points to it. "This is a square. Say it."	"Square!"
"Great!" Draws another square, larger than the previous two, using a third color of marker. Points to it. "This is a square. Say it."	"Square!"
"Awesome!" Points to a square previously drawn. "What is it?"	"Square!"
"Amazing!" Points to another. "And this is a . . . ?	"Square!"
"Superb!" Draws a rectangle on the board. Points to it. "This is NOT a square. Say 'Not a square.'"	"Not a square!"
"Perfect." Draws a circle on the board. Points to it. "This is NOT a square. Say it."	"Not a square!"
"Amazing!" Points to a square previously drawn. "Is this a square? Say Yes or No."	"Yes!"
"Fantastic!" Points to the rectangle. "Is this a square? Say Yes or No."	"No!"
"Exactly!" Draws a heart on the board. Points to it. "Is this a square or not a square?"	"Not a square!"
"Perfecto!" Draws an oval on the board. Points to it. "Is this a square or not a square?"	"Not a square!"
"Awesome!" Points to a square on the board. "Is this a square or not a square?"	"Square!"

The lesson described above requires less than five minutes of teaching time and, in that short period, all of the students in her class have effectively learned the concept of "square." Let's evaluate the essential components of the lesson one by one. The teacher constructed a *faultless communication* by 1) first presenting the positive example (i.e., square) in three different sizes drawn in three different colors to rule out the possibility of miscommunicating that size or color are aspects of the concept of square, 2) juxtaposing a negative example sharing similar characteristics (i.e., rectangle) in close proximity to the positive examples of square to emphasize the critical features of square (i.e., four *equal* sides), 3) juxtaposing positive and negative examples throughout the lesson to solidify discrimination of the concept, and 4) providing immediate and enthusiastic feedback for every response given by the class.

Moreover, the teacher kept her presentations very brief rather than inundating her students with lots of words. However, even inside of these brief presentations, she varied her question types in such a way that the class could engage in *flexible* responding such as answering with "square," "not a square," "yes," or "no." This type of flexibility capitalizes on relational responding regarding sameness and difference, enhances attention, and promotes generalization of the concept. She also promoted flexibility in responding without using the actual names of the other shapes included as negative examples. She increased the faultlessness of her communication because she did not introduce additional concepts that could have created miscommunications or confusion for those learners without a preexisting knowledge of other shapes. It is very possible to teach the concept of "square" in relation to other shapes without actually using the names of those other shapes at all. The learner simply has to frame an example as "square" or "not square" to effectively learn the concept. It's brilliant in its simplicity!

She also required that the entire class respond in unison to every question she presented rather than having the class raise their hands and give only the chosen student the opportunity to actively respond and have that response reinforced. The entire class was provided the opportunity to respond to every question presented in the lesson. Thus, every child in the class was behaving with respect to the subject matter, and that behavior was being subsequently reinforced by the teacher.

Finally, and this aspect of effective DI instruction cannot be gleaned from the example provided above, a well-trained DI instructor presents stimuli and questions at a rapid pace. Empirical studies of this method clearly point to the beneficial effects of rapid pacing during a lesson. Another one of the myths floating around is that in order for children to learn, teachers must present materials slowly. This notion is categorically false. Effective instruction involves rapid pacing, choral responding, immediate feedback, and faultless communications of concepts.[104]

Teaching Concepts: An Example from the Establishment

Now, let's compare the DI method of teaching the concept of "square" with the kind of lesson a traditional educator would likely design. Obviously, the lesson example I am providing is a hypothetical, but its construction is based on the tenets of progressive education and the types of lessons I have observed traditional educators use in the teaching of concepts like "square."

TEACHER	CLASS
"Today we are going to talk about a very special shape. There are lots of shapes. Can anyone tell me the name of a shape they have learned?" Pauses, looks around class for a student to raise their hand.	Some students raise their hands. Others stare at the teacher without raising their hands. Others fidget, scribble, stare out the window, mess with their neighbor, look in their desks, etc.
Several seconds have elapsed. "OK, Sally, can you tell me the name of a shape you know?"	Sally only: "A circle"

TEACHER	CLASS
"Great—a circle is a shape. But we are not going to talk about circles today. Who else can tell me a shape they know?"	Some students raise their hands. Others stare at the teacher without raising their hands. Others fidget, scribble, stare out the window, mess with their neighbor, look in their desks, etc.
Several more seconds have elapsed. "Johnny, what shape do you know?"	Johnny only: "A triangle"
"OK—good! We aren't going to talk about triangles today. We are going to talk about another shape. Can anyone guess what shape we might be talking about? I'll give you some hints. It's the shape of our window, our bookcase, part of the house we have on the bulletin board. Can anyone guess what that shape is?"	Some students raise their hands. Others stare at the teacher without raising their hands. Others fidget, scribble, stare out the window, mess with their neighbor, look in their desks, etc.
More seconds pass. "Brittany, what shape do you think it is?"	Brittany only: "A rectangle?"
"No—not a rectangle. Our door is a rectangle. The area of the floor that we are sitting in right now is a rectangle. My desk is a rectangle. We aren't talking about rectangles. What shape might we be talking about?"	Some students raise their hands. Others stare at the teacher without raising their hands. Others fidget, scribble, stare out the window, mess with their neighbor, look in their desks, etc.
More seconds pass. "Samantha, what shape do you think it is?"	Samantha only: "A square?"
"Yes! Great job! We are going to talk about squares today. Who can find some squares in the room? What things in our room are shaped like squares?"	Some students raise their hands. Others stare at the teacher without raising their hand. Others fidget, scribble, stare out the window, mess with their neighbor, look in their desks, etc.

I will stop there because on and on lessons of this sort go. The entire class period will continue in this manner with the end result being that a majority of the class will *not* have learned the concept of "square." The students who came to class that day already knowing what a square is will be fine, though their learning didn't happen on that teacher's watch. However, what about the students who did not come to class knowing what a square is? What about the students who failed to learn this concept? What about those learners who failed to engage in the lesson at all because they were not in fact required or simply *encouraged* to engage in it? These are the types of lessons and teaching practices that dominate our nation's schools. These practices are tragically ineffective; yet, when learners fail to learn under these ridiculously poor conditions, it is the learner who is blamed for this failure.

The type of lesson presented in the above example can in no way be described as *faultless.* The failure of the class to learn the concept of square is clearly the fault of the teacher's poor communication, not some inherent disability of the learners in the class who happened to come to school needing to learn the concept of square rather than being lucky enough to already know it. Yet, students in our nation's schools are expected to learn under these abysmal conditions every day without a consideration of the impact those conditions have on the learners who are their victims. The lucky few students who make it successfully through our nation's education system do so *despite* that education, not as a result of it.

The Myth of the Socratic Method

You will notice that the DI instructor began her lesson by *telling* her students the correct answer. In other words, she drew a square, pointed to it, said "This is a square," instructed her students to say "square" in unison, and provided immediate reinforcement for this response. Such a practice is blasphemy to the educational establishment! Teachers are trained to believe that nothing should be directly instructed in this way. Children should be provided with opportunities to explore and discover the correct answers for themselves. The teacher should serve only as their gentle guide. Many parents who have been sold the progressive ideology think that this notion sounds very romantic and idyllic. They imagine their children exploring, imagining, and creating in the classroom—discovering the laws or principles of the universe for themselves.

This notion stems from the ancient Socratic method where a pupil is merely guided to the correct answer through a series of questions.[133] It is unclear to me how an ancient Greek method of instruction has become synonymous with *progressive* education, but that is the method primarily used in our nation's schools. An ancient Greek method without any empirical support whatsoever. I need only provide you with one very simple example of the difference in efficiency and effectiveness between a lesson based on the empirically validated tenets of DI versus one informed by the ideology of progressive education. In the DI method, five minutes is all it took to actively engage an entire class of youngsters in the effective learning of a concept. In the other, during the same five minutes, all that took place was a few students answering questions that were completely unrelated to the actual concept in the lesson. The majority of the class was disengaged, with no real learning taking place.

The bottom line is that children attend school to learn what they *do not* already know! It has taken the human race thousands of years to make the discoveries that we must pass down to our children via instruction. We have a lot to teach and very little time to teach it. We honestly do not have the time to allow children to discover concepts like fractions for themselves! It is simply not possible for a small child to discover for themselves what it has taken humans centuries to discover. How does such a method make any sense at all? We must tell students the answers and provide them the opportunity to master skills and concepts in such a way that they can get into the business of making *new* discoveries that will advance the human race. We can't waste time hoping that they will make old discoveries. We need them to make *new* ones! They must master preexisting knowledge quickly and effectively, so that the old knowledge can be built upon in the service of moving forward to discover new knowledge.

Discovering new knowledge by building upon the old is the very definition of progress. "Progressive education is actually *regressive* education."[4] We must declare that we refuse to base our educational system on going backward. We must move forward! What is more exciting than an engaged group of youngsters being quickly and effectively instructed in all of the amazing discoveries made by humanity with the intention that, eventually, those very youngsters will become the new great discoverers of vital aspects of our world who will contribute to the further advancement and survival of the human race? To me, that sounds a lot like progress.

Curriculum-Based Measurement

Precision Teaching is a measurement system based in natural science that enables teachers to precisely and reliably evaluate learning. Proximal measurement practices like these involve the daily measurement of directly targeted skills as well as frequent monitoring of generative gains made on related, untargeted skills. At Fit Learning, as learners are engaging in deliberate, purposeful practice of skills, we are also regularly checking their performance on related but unpracticed skills to identify if generative gains are being produced. Such practices are essential components of the Technology of Teaching.

However, as important to the Technology of Teaching are more *distal* measurement practices, so that broad-scale gains toward a more distant goal are also consistently monitored—such as gains on standard academic achievement measures. Fit Learning combines the proximal measurement of daily targets with the measurement of more distal targets through the use of Curriculum-Based Measurement

(CBM). CBM is a national assessment method with over 30 years of research supporting its reliability and validity at predicting long-term academic success.[134-136] Although stemming from the field of education, CBM has been heavily influenced by behavioral science. CBM arose as an "effort to decrease the separation between measurement and instruction." [134] CBM assessments are designed directly from the classroom curriculum and are administered daily, weekly, or at other benchmark periods throughout the school year. There are many digital platforms, such as AimsWeb, that provide teachers with the necessary assessment materials across many academic domains such as reading, math, spelling, handwriting, expressive writing, and so forth.[137]

In CBM, as in Precision Teaching, learner performance is measured directly, and performance is displayed graphically with calendar time on the horizontal axis as with the Standard Celeration Chart. AimsWeb also provides digital graphing platforms for teachers where they input their students' assessment scores and a graph is immediately generated for each student. Educators gain a time-series display of student progress enabling instructional decision-making. In this way, CBM is individually referenced, so that students' current performance can be compared with respect to their own past performance.

The CBM research program has led to the national norm-referencing of thousands of learners, so that assessment performance can also be evaluated with respect to percentile rank. In this way, individual student performance can be compared with performance by peers within a classroom, school, or district. Through this more distal lens, progress on proximal targets can be compared with percentile rank gains on more global targets. As with the expanded proximal lens, comparisons between proximal and distal gains provide educators with the opportunity to discover important functional relations between specific instructional variables and their broad-scale impact on learning for each individual student as well as across students, schools, and districts.

At Fit Learning, we plot the rate of responding on individual SCCs for each skill we are targeting during training. For example, each skill identified on our comprehensive skills assessment as below the fluency aim is subsequently introduced into training through repeated, reinforced practice. So a reading student may be practicing component skills for reading during each session such as identifying letter sounds, identifying phonetic rules through DI instruction, and applying phonetic rules for decoding words. In addition to plotting their rates of responding on SCCs for each of these component skills, we also conduct weekly CBM assessments to evaluate their increasing percentile ranks on standardized measures of reading achievement. In this way, we can reliably determine if their increasing fluency on component reading skills is leading to generative gains being made on grade-level reading skills as measured by CBM reading assessments.

By combining these proximal and distal measurement practices, we have discovered that by building fluency on component skills, we reliably produce dramatic increases on standard academic achievement measures. Fit Learning produces increases of more than 30 percentile ranks in 40 hours of instruction on CBM assessments. In other words, we produce close to a percentile rank gain per hour of instruction on standard measures of academic achievement. These are exponentially greater gains than most American students make in an entire school year, and we produce them in as little as 40 hours of instruction.

THE TECHNOLOGY OF TEACHING IN THE CLASSROOM

The Technology of Teaching combines behavioral science, Precision Teaching (PT), Direct Instruction (DI), and Curriculum-Based Measurement (CBM) into one highly effective method. Using the Technology of Teaching, Fit Learning has produced over one year's growth in only 40 hours of training with thousands of even the most challenged learners worldwide. We adhere to the principles of learning and behavioral science for the design of our instructional practices and the implementation of these practices with every student enrolled. We utilize PT to evaluate the immediate effectiveness of our instruction and determine when mastery of skills has been achieved. We utilize DI for the construction of faultless communications for our instruction of concepts to be learned and mastered. We utilize CBM to evaluate distal gains on global, grade-level targets in relation to the achievement of fluency in essential component skills.

This Technology of Teaching can also be implemented in the classroom.[2, 3, 9, 13, 117, 118, 134, 136, 138–143] In the example of teaching "square" provided above, a classroom teacher combining these approaches would follow her efficient and effective DI lesson in the concept of square with timed practice in identifying squares, such as having her students mark the squares from a series of shapes presented on worksheets. Although her concept instruction was highly effective, it is not enough to ensure true mastery of the concept. So after a quick concept lesson, students would engage in some sort of "deliberate, purposeful" practice of this concept by engaging in timed practice with reinforcement delivered for the achievement of Personal Best goals.

Contrary to popular belief, timed practice can actually be implemented with groups of students. The teacher begins a timer for the class and the students work vigorously throughout the timing period. At the end of the timing, students can check their work, write their count correct and incorrect in a space provided on their worksheets, and declare the achievement of PBs. The teacher can then deliver reinforcement for goal achievement and encouraging statements and instructional strategies to those students who failed to achieve their PBs. The teacher can then begin another practice timing so that her students have the opportunity to try again and improve their performance. In less than 10 minutes, her class has received effective concept instruction *and* fluency-based practice of this concept. At the end of the lesson, the teacher can collect her students' practice data and record it on individual Standard Celeration Charts (SCCs) so that she can monitor the individual learning of every student in her class. With the development of digital charting platforms such as Chartlytics, charting and analyzing learning data for children in a classroom has become a very efficient process.[103]

The teacher could also design *tests* for generative learning gains in relation to the deliberate, purposeful practice of directly trained skills. In the square example above, a generativity check might entail a timing with learners running about the room to find as many squares as possible, tallying each square they identify. The teacher could collect these data and chart them on generativity SCCs for each student.

Practice of this sort continues over time until each student has achieved the fluency goal indicative of mastery for that concept. Some students are going to master the skill more quickly than others. Again, variability is the very nature of human learning! Those students who achieve mastery of a skill can move on to a new concept while other students who need more time to master the previous skill can keep practicing it. In evaluating her students' SCCs, the teacher can determine whether certain students require interventions to increase their celerations so that their learning occurs at a faster rate and mastery of skills occurs more quickly. Such interventions might involve further instruction of the concept, changing or increasing reinforcement for Personal Best goals, shortening of timings lengths to sprints before gradually increasing them again, changing learning materials in some way, and so on.

By adhering to the principles of learning and behavioral science, teachers have access to science-based strategies in the design of instructional interventions. In this sense, her class will involve grouping students according to their own pace and this grouping will depend on the skill or concept being mastered. The teacher will be individualizing instruction for every learner in her class, ensuring that, although she must teach a large group of students, her instruction occurs based on each student as an individual.

On a weekly basis, the teacher could conduct CBM assessments with her class to obtain a distal measure of progress toward more global, grade-level standards. These CBM data can also be charted on individual SCCs for each student using Chartlytics or through the use of the graphing platform offered by AimsWeb. In this way, she can monitor the progress of each student in her class toward grade-level standards in relation to the component skills being learned, practiced, and mastered in the classroom. Immediate instructional decisions can be made regarding her students' progress in relation to both proximal and distal targets.

I have just described the Technology of Teaching for the classroom, a system of instruction based in behavioral science and the principles of learning. The Technology of Teaching is scientifically sound and technically precise. This is a viable answer to our current educational crisis. This technology has been systematically ignored and blocked by the establishment for decades. We can no longer accept the establishment's refusal to evolve. We can no longer allow our educational system to remain an ideological one entrenched in a belief system that prevents progress and sentences children to lifetimes of mediocrity and failure.

Our children have a fundamental right to an effective, science-based education. Our teachers have a fundamental right to receive training in science-based instruction so they can effectively carry out the job they are all expected to perform. As citizens, we have the right to an educated public capable of devising innovative solutions to the many problems we face as a nation and a species. These are fundamental rights of every American. We must all demand that our teachers be trained in the Technology of Teaching and that this technology be implemented in all of our nation's schools. We must demand it and we must demand it *now*.

7

THE EVIDENCE

*"Meaningful school reform will not be achieved
until we acknowledge that how well students learn
is a function of how they are taught."*
—CATHY WATKINS[8]

Up to this point, I have made a lot of claims about the profound effectiveness of behavioral science and the Technology of Teaching. It is time for me to put my money where my mouth is. Let's review the evidence demonstrating the superiority of instructional practices guided by behavioral science. Again, the evidence I am presenting is in no way exhaustive. I encourage you to consult all the references I have provided if you wish to expand your knowledge beyond the scope of this book.

Some of the evidence I am going to describe reflects large-scale studies. The rest reflects program evaluations conducted at Fit Learning, where we have aggregated outcome data produced with thousands of our learners through applied science. This evidence was not collected via controlled studies but produced in the course of our work with kids, which, as I previously described, entails conducting applied natural science with every learner. Doing so allows us to evaluate whether the methods we use produce measurable gains on both proximal and distal targets. These are the kinds of programmatic analyses that could be conducted by all of our nation's schools through the Technology of Teaching. That would provide a collective database of best practices, which would finally enable our schools to evolve.

PROJECT FOLLOW THROUGH

To this day, Project Follow Through is the largest and most expensive federally funded study of educational methods ever conducted in America.[8] Launched in 1965, it evaluated 21 different educational methods, including two based in behavioral science: The Direct Instruction Model and the Behavior Analysis Model. Results of this 10-year study unequivocally demonstrated the superiority of the two methods based in behavioral science, with Direct Instruction outperforming *all other models* by at least two standard deviations on standardized tests of academic achievement as well as measures of self-esteem.

The other models included in Project Follow Through reflected the ideology of progressive education and the educational establishment. Results indicated that many of these models actually led to *decreases* in both achievement scores and measures of self-esteem. In other words, many students receiving this kind of instruction actually worsened over time. So we have empirical evidence going back to the 1960s that instruction based on progressive ideologies fundamentally does not work, and even more alarming, has the potential to make academic performance and self-esteem *worse*. How does that sit with you?

The results of Project Follow Through set off a flurry of evidence-gathering activities by the establishment. They brought in different data analysis companies in an attempt to reconfigure results in various ways to change the findings in support of progressive methods. None of these attempts were successful in changing the results. No matter how they tried to reanalyze the data, instruction based on behavioral science came out on top.

When this strategy didn't work, the establishment attempted to delegitimize the achievement tests that were used and claim that the kinds of measures included in a scientific study could never capture the true goals of education: education of the whole child. As a result of this entrenched dogmatism, they persuaded Congress to eliminate funding for the effective, behaviorally based methods and increase funding for the ineffective methods that matched the ideology of the educational establishment, even though those very methods had not only failed to educate kids but had actually left many of them *less* educated. And here we are today, with more than 60% of all students, 80% of minority and low-income students, and 90% of students classified as LD graduating below proficiency in all academic subjects. Project Follow Through provides the clearest example of the dangers of ideology in an institution that should operate from the perspective of scientific inquiry and pragmatism. Ideology blocks progress and ensures that such institutions never evolve.

THE GREAT FALLS PRECISION TEACHING PROJECT

In the 1960s, behavioral scientists began applying the principles of learning and the process of natural science in applied settings.[59, 144–146] Our friend Ogden Lindsley was a student of B. F. Skinner, and he was one of the first to bring basic behavioral science out of the laboratory and into the applied setting. As I previously stated, he developed Precision Teaching (PT) and the Standard Celeration Chart (SCC) to place the same scientific tools used in the laboratory into the hands of teachers, to give them the power to make the same kinds of discoveries regarding learning and behavior as those made through our basic science.[121] Since that time, hundreds of thousands of charts reflecting applied natural science have been collected and analyzed in applied settings — classrooms included.[147] As a result, vast discoveries have been made regarding the design of learning environments and instructional practices that rapidly accelerate learning gains with every type of learner.

In the early 1970s, the first large-scale study of PT was conducted in Great Falls, Montana.[9] This initial study was conducted over a four-year period in the Sacajewea Elementary School, where teachers were trained to implement PT practices with students in their classrooms. The effects of those methods were evaluated by comparing Sacajewea students with those students in the district receiving traditional instruction. Results demonstrated that the Sacajewea students, who received only 20 to 30 minutes of PT per day, outperformed other students in the district by an average of 19 to 40 percentile points on the Iowa Test of Basic Skills. As a result, the Joint Review Panel of the U.S. Office of Education extended the study to include other schools in the Great Falls school district, which resulted in findings that students participating in PT advanced an average of two or more grade levels per year compared with students in traditional education, many of whom failed to advance even one grade level per year.

Since that study, these findings have been consistently replicated by schools utilizing PT methods, such as Morningside Academy in Seattle, as well as by learning centers like Fit Learning.[11] In other words, since the 1960s, PT has been shown to consistently produce exponentially greater learning gains than traditional approaches. Yet these findings have been continuously ignored or erroneously refuted by the educational establishment.

FIT LEARNING

Pragmatic institutions continually evolve by conducting science, evaluating results, adopting practices, and discarding others based on that science. Fit Learning is one such pragmatic institution, which is why for over 20 years, we have continually evolved and improved our methods. Learners enrolled with us today improve even more dramatically than learners enrolled with us as recently as two years ago, because we are constantly evolving through scientific inquiry.

To reiterate, Fit Learning combines behavioral science, Precision Teaching, Direct Instruction, and Curriculum-Based Measurement (CBM) into a Technology of Teaching that results in the rapid acceleration of learning gains. We conduct applied natural science with each student, systematically evaluating learning gains on proximal targets (i.e., core skills targeted for fluency during training) in relation to growth on untargeted distal, grade-level targets (i.e., CBM assessments). The applied science we do at the individual learner level is then aggregated into large-scale programmatic outcome analyses of all learners enrolled at all of our locations. Fit Learning currently has more than 30 locations operating worldwide with hundreds of learners enrolled each year. We obtain and evaluate large amounts of process-level as well as program-level data for use in analyzing and improving our methods.

Process-Level Analyses

Our process-level analyses occur as the act of instruction itself. We initially conduct a comprehensive skills assessment with every learner to identify deficient skills that need to be trained to fluency. We then generate a fluency-building program for each student to target deficient skills. As we conduct sessions with learners, we collect rate data for each skill performed, chart those data on individual SCCs for every skill, manipulate variables related to instruction in a systematic manner, and evaluate the manipulation of those variables over time with respect to learning and mastery. We also conduct weekly CBM assessments to monitor our students' growth on more distal achievement measures.

After our learners have received 40 hours of training, we re-administer the comprehensive skills assessment to evaluate gains in accuracy and fluency across all prerequisite skills included in the specific academic domain being targeted during sessions. We also conduct additional CBM assessments at every 40-hour benchmark to evaluate percentile rank gains made on academic achievement measures related to the component skills being targeted during sessions. We follow this process with each of our learners—including Alex, who I have mentioned often in this book. To illustrate how this process works for an individual learner, I have included figures reflecting Alex's Reading Skills Assessments as well as his CBM Reading Assessments in the appendix for this chapter.

Program Analysis: Lab Level

We also conduct program-level analyses of our outcomes produced across learners by aggregating their 40-hour comprehensive skills assessment data and CBM data for each Fit Learning location, which we call learning laboratories or labs. I have included an example of this type of program-level analysis at the lab level in the appendix for this chapter, with figures reflecting aggregate Reading Skills Assessments and CBM Reading Assessments conducted with 54 learners enrolled in our tristate locations, which include Locust Valley, New York; New York City; and Greenwich, Connecticut.

Program Analysis: Organizational Level

Finally, we conduct program-level analyses of our outcomes by aggregating 40-hour CBM assessments conducted with all learners across all learning labs in our organization. Here I am going to share aggregate outcomes obtained with our learners through 2019.

The figures that follow reflect 40-hour percentile rank gains obtained on CBM assessments conducted with all of our learners across all Fit Learning laboratories worldwide. For each figure, the number of CBM assessments aggregated in each column on the figure is reflected by the "N" size indicated at the top of the figure. This "N" applies to the number of assessments included in each Intake and 40-hour column. In other words, the same learners were assessed at Intake and at 40 hours, so each column reflects that same "N" size. Additionally, learners may have had multiple assessments conducted at Intake and 40 hours, which is why the "N" reflects the number of assessments conducted rather than the number of learners assessed. The first column on each figure reflects our learners' average percentile rank at their Intake assessment, which takes place prior to enrollment. The second column reflects our learners' average percentile rank following 40 hours of training at Fit Learning.

To clarify, percentile rank refers to how a student performs in relation to other students nationally. For example, a student scoring in the 25th percentile performed better than only 25% of students nationally. A student scoring in the 50th percentile performed better than 50% of students nationally. A student scoring in the 75th percentile performed better than 75% of students nationally. In this sense, percentile ranks reflect a "normal" distribution of scores with the 25th percentile reflecting the lower quartile, 50th percentile reflecting the middle quartile, and 75th percentile reflecting the upper quartile. In a normal distribution, the upper and lower quartiles form the high and low "tails," and the middle quartile forms the wider "bell" part of the distribution. The bell curve shape of a normal distribution reflects that a majority of students score under the "bell" and a smaller percentage of students score in the high and low "tails." AimsWeb provided all of the CBM assessments conducted with our learners along with information regarding their national percentile rank.[137]

Aggregate Gains Across All CBM Assessments

Figure 5 reflects improvements in percentile rank on 1,978 CBM assessments conducted at Intake and after 40 hours of training with learners across all of our locations. These assessments involved all academic domains: reading and math readiness, oral reading fluency, reading comprehension, math computation, complex mathematical problem-solving, written expression, and spelling.

On average, our learners scored in the 27th percentile at Intake, prior to their enrollment at Fit Learning (reflected by the Intake

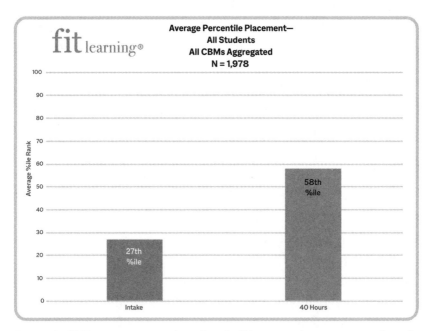

Figure 5. *CBM assessments conducted with all learners. Assessments conducted include reading (R-CBM), reading comprehension (CBM MAZE), math algorithms (M-COMP), complex math (M-CAP), CBM Spelling, CBM Correct Writing Sequence, CBM Tests of Early Literacy, and CBM Tests of Early Numeracy.*

column). Thus, our learners performed in the bottom quartile of students nationally before receiving any training from us. Following 40 hours of training, our learners increased to the 58th percentile across all CBM assessments (reflected by the 40 hours column). Therefore, our learners moved from the bottom quartile to the top half of students nationally in only 40 hours of training. On average, our students gained 31 percentile ranks, which reflects more than one year of academic growth in just 40 hours of training.

Fit Reading

We can also look at average percentile rank gain obtained for specific academic domains. Figure 6 reflects gains obtained on 348 R-CBM assessments, an assessment of oral reading fluency. This assessment measures a learner's reading mechanics, or the ability to decode and

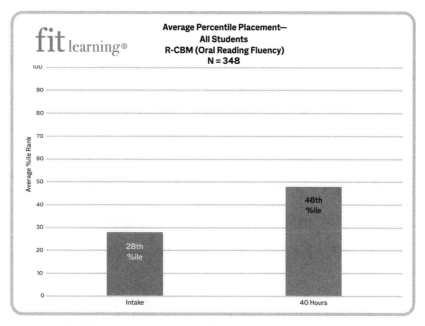

Figure 6. R-CBM assessments conducted with all learners. R-CBM evaluates oral reading fluency.

read words as well as read text with prosody—high quality reading that resembles the pace of natural speech. To clarify, this CBM assessment evaluates only a learner's reading rate, or how many words they can read per minute. This assessment does not evaluate comprehension of reading material.

On average, our learners increased from the 28th percentile to the 48th percentile on an assessment of oral reading fluency. Our learners gained an average of 20 percentile ranks following 40 hours of training in phonemic awareness, decoding, and the mechanics of reading.

Figure 7 reflects gains obtained on 271 CBM Maze assessments, a measure of reading comprehension.

On average, our learners increased from the 26th percentile to the 59th percentile on the Maze assessment. Our learners gained 33 percentile ranks in 40 hours of training on an assessment of

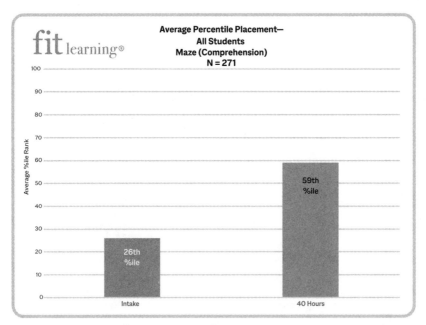

Figure 7. CBM MAZE assessments conducted with all learners. CBM MAZE evaluates reading comprehension.

reading comprehension. These gains were obtained with learners who received instruction mainly in phonemic awareness, decoding, and the mechanics of reading. By improving our learners' decoding skills and general reading fluency, we were able to produce *generative* gains in reading comprehension. As a result of becoming better readers, our learners collaterally got better at understanding what they were reading.

Fit Math

Figure 8 reflects gains obtained on 225 M-COMP assessments, which measures solving math algorithms involving addition, subtraction, multiplication, division, fractions, and decimals.

On average, our learners increased from the 29th percentile to the 64th percentile on the M-COMP assessment. Our learners gained

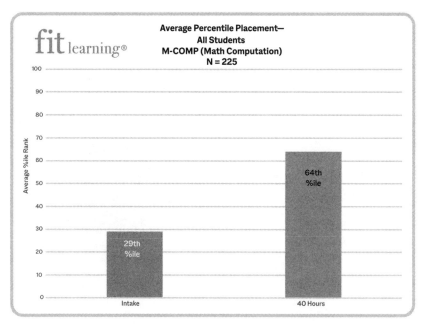

Figure 8. M-COMP assessments conducted with all learners. M-COMP evaluates math computation.

35 percentile ranks after 40 hours of training in basic numeracy and computation skills.

Figure 9 reflects gains obtained on 173 M-CAP assessments, which measure more complex applications of mathematics like solving word problems as well as problems involving graphs and figures.

On average, our learners increased from the 30th percentile to the 70th percentile on the M-CAP assessment. Our learners gained 40 percentile ranks in 40 hours of training in basic math skills. Similar to our outcomes for reading comprehension, our M-CAP scores reflect generative or collateral gains produced with learners who mainly received training in core numeracy and computation skills. In other words, after 40 hours of training in core math skills, our learners were able to apply those skills for the solving of complex language-based math problems.

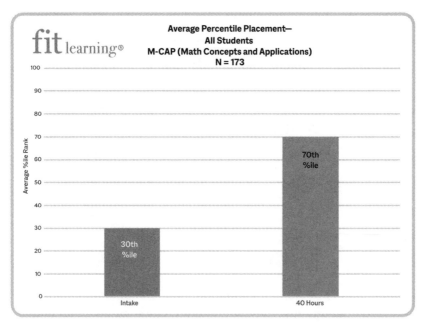

Figure 9. M-CAP assessments conducted with all learners. M-CAP evaluates concepts and applications of mathematics.

Moreover, our learners enrolled scoring close to the *bottom quartile* of students nationally, but after only 40 hours of training in core math skills, our learners had increased close to the *top quartile* of students nationally. Again, these gains were not achieved by targeting these more complex math skills. They were achieved by producing fluency in prerequisite numeracy and computations skills — those skills that the establishment wants our nation's schools to skip over.

Lil Fits: Early Learners (PreK–K)

We also produce these kinds of profound gains with very young learners enrolled in our Lil Fits program, which targets academic readiness and learning to learn skills with 3-to 5-year- old children. Figure 10 reflects gains obtained on 735 Tests of Early Literacy and

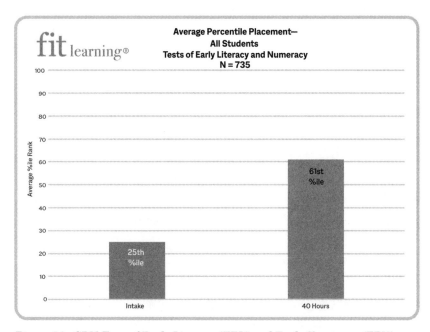

Figure 10. CBM Tests of Early Literacy (TEL) and Early Numeracy (TEN) conducted with all learners. TEL and TEN evaluate early literacy and numeracy skills.

Numeracy, which evaluate young learners' abilities to engage in early academic skills such as identifying phonics, decoding basic words, identifying numbers, counting in sequence, and so forth.

On average, our very young learners increased from the 25th percentile to the 61st percentile on Tests of Early Literacy and Numeracy. Our young learners gained an average of 36 percentile ranks in 40 hours of training.

As with our older learners, our young learners tested in the bottom quartile of students nationally at intake but moved to the top half of students nationally after 40 hours of training. Moreover, many of the gains achieved with these young learners were also achieved *collaterally*. In other words, the training they received in their initial 40 hours involved strengthening their looking and listening skills, increasing their compliance, strengthening their relational language skills, and increasing their fluency for identifying letter names and sounds. By simply strengthening their ability to learn and giving them a foundation in phonics, these learners were able to engage in more complex academic skills with little to no training.

The establishments maintain that children acquire academic and cognitive skills as a result of their physical development or age. However, the outcomes we achieve with our young learners clearly contradict these beliefs. They indicate that children acquire skills through effective instruction, regardless of age. Learning can be rapidly accelerated with any learner through the design of instruction based on behavioral science and the Technology of Teaching.

Students Classified as LD

We can also evaluate our outcomes for those learners classified as LD. Figure 11 reflects percentile rank gains across 731 CBM assessments conducted with our learners classified with various learning disabilities such as ADD, dyslexia, autism, processing disorders, and so on.

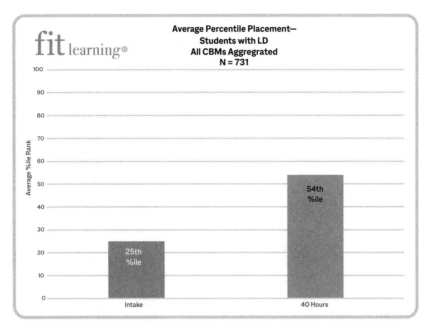

Figure 11. CBM assessments conducted with learners who are classified as learning disabled (LD). Assessments conducted include R-CBM, CBM MAZE, M-COMP, M-CAP, CBM Spelling, CBM Correct Writing Sequence, CBM Tests of Early Literacy, and CBM Tests of Early Numeracy.

The figure reflects that, on average, our learners classified as LD increased from the 25th percentile to the 54th percentile across all academic assessments conducted. Our classified learners gained an average of 29 percentile ranks in 40 hours of training. Let's compare these gains to the outcomes we produce with learners who are not classified as LD.

Figure 12 reflects percentile rank gains obtained across 1,262 CBM assessments conducted with our non-classified learners.

The figure reflects that, on average, our non-classified learners increased from the 28th percentile to the 60th percentile across all academic assessments conducted. As such, our non-classified students gained 32 percentile ranks in 40 hours of training. In comparison, our

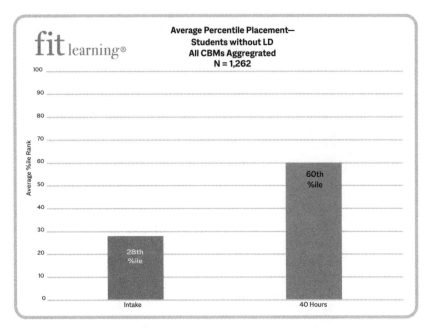

Figure 12. CBM assessments conducted with non-classified learners. Assessments conducted include R-CBM, CBM MAZE, M-COMP, M-CAP, CBM Spelling, CBM Correct Writing Sequence, CBM Tests of Early Literacy, and CBM Tests of Early Numeracy.

classified students gained 29 percentile ranks in 40 hours of training. These outcomes indicate that our non-classified learners gained only three more percentile ranks than our learners classified as LD. In other words, our classified and non-classified learners made similar gains on measures of academic achievement.

The outcomes we produce with learners classified as LD support my assertion that failure to learn results from faulty learning environments, not something faulty within the learner. On average, our LD learners made significantly more gains in academic achievement than the average American student makes in an entire school year. Their ability to learn was astounding, as it is with all of our learners. With instruction guided by behavioral science and the Technology of

Teaching it is possible to produce dramatic gains in academic achievement with every type of learner, regardless of a classification they may have been given.

THE MYTH OF NORMAL DISTRIBUTIONS

I have previously mentioned that achievement test scores create normal distributions, where a majority of learners score under the bell and fewer students score in the high and low tails. It is widely believed that these distributions reflect the normal distribution in aptitude of learners. In other words, the establishments assert that these tests measure characteristics of students that are immutable or fixed traits, where a large number of students are born with average abilities and a much smaller number are born with very high or very low abilities. The establishments have led the public to believe that these distributions represent natural variation in human aptitude, which has absolutely nothing to do with instruction.

The behavioral methods used in the Follow Through study, the Great Falls study, and by Fit Learning all resulted in moving a distribution of achievement scores. In each example, achievement scores shifted upward by significant amounts. With respect to the outcome data from Fit Learning, prior to enrollment, our learners scored in the low tails of a normal distribution: the bottom quartile. Following 40 hours of instruction, those same learners had moved to the middle or upper quartiles of that distribution. Students attend school for about seven hours per day, which accumulates to about 35 hours per week. So in 40 hours, about the time of a typical school week, we were able to improve our learners' academic achievement by 20 to 40 percentile ranks, significantly more gain than most American students make in an entire school year.

Normal distributions of academic achievement do not reflect natural variation in human aptitude; they reflect the outcomes of the instructional practices being used. A majority of students score as average because, at best, traditional educational practices result in mediocre achievement. Our NAEP scores indicate that a majority of students fail to acquire proficiency and less than 10% achieve the advanced level in any academic subject. These abysmal scores have nothing to do with human aptitude and everything to do with ineffective teaching practices.

Instruction based on behavioral science and the Technology of Teaching has been empirically validated since the 1960s and has consistently produced exponentially greater levels of academic achievement than methods based on the ideologies of the educational establishment. For close to 60 years, a Technology of Teaching has existed as a solution to our educational crisis. Yet this technology has never been widely implemented because it does not match the beliefs of the establishment. Our educational system has never evolved, and it never will unless we all demand that it begins to operate as a pragmatic institution rather than an ideological one.

8

THE FUTURE

"We're all in this together."
—CHUCK MERBITZ

Where do we go from here? Now that you have met the various establishments, traditions, and myths that dominate our nation's schools and have been introduced to behavioral science and the Technology of Teaching as an alternative, what are we going to do about it? In the beginning of this book, I suggested that moving forward might require you to experience a bit of discomfort—go through a detox, if you will—as you let go of some of the beliefs that feed these establishments. So, what am I actually asking you to give up?

Let's start with what I'm *not* asking you to give up. I'm not asking you to give up your religion. I'm not asking you to give up your mysticism or magic. I'm not asking you to give up your identity or personality or that of your children. I'm not asking you to give up any of the characteristics that ultimately make you or your children unique—that ultimately make us all human. Quite the contrary. If religion provides you with comfort, then I want you to have that comfort. If magic or mysticism entertain you or help you get through the day, then I want you to have that too.

What I am asking you to consider is the possibility that sometimes our beliefs get in the way. Sometimes our beliefs prevent us from making progress, from being effective, from solving problems that really need to be solved for the betterment, not only of our own lives, but of all humanity. Is it possible to hold on to your beliefs but be willing to let go when doing so might make a difference? I think it is possible and I think pragmatism is what makes it possible.

Behavioral scientists are pragmatists. A pragmatist is someone who values being effective. Above all else, we value making a difference, and we have discovered that our science enables us to make that difference. From a pragmatic perspective, our methods are evaluated in terms of whether or not they effectively accomplish our goals: adjusting the environment in a way that changes behavior and improves the quality of life.

In contrast, from an ideological perspective, methods are evaluated in terms of whether they cohere with *beliefs.* Ideology gets us into a lot of trouble in areas of human life where being effective is of great importance. When beliefs run the show, we gather evidence to verify our beliefs and tend to ignore or attempt to refute evidence that conflicts with what we believe. In other words, we are on a constant quest for agreement so that we can prove ourselves *right.* Our need for agreement can lead us down a dangerously dogmatic path, which ultimately blocks progress and prevents us from being open to change.

Dogmatism and self-righteousness can also stem from a lack of awareness that alternative perspectives exist. As I stated in the introduction, I wrote this book to uncover your *blind spots.* To uncover for you the many things *you didn't know that you didn't know* about the ineffectiveness of our educational system and the real reasons why students fail. The establishments fill the airwaves with all kinds of explanations for systemic academic failure, like pointing to the increasing prevalence of learning disabilities or other inherent characteristics of students that contribute to their being largely "uneducable."

The establishments also offer explanations that reflect top-down issues like a lack of school funds, the need for privatization and school choice, too much or too little administrative oversight, teacher shortages, overcrowded classrooms, and a lack of necessary materials and resources. I think we can all agree that schools require sufficient funding to operate properly. We also need enough teachers and school supplies to go around. However, all of the reasons for failure offered by the establishments fail to address the fundamental problem: teaching practices don't work.

I hope at this point you have discovered your blind spots around the actual reasons why so many students fail. Students fail because they advance through the grade levels according to age rather than true mastery of prerequisite skills. Students fail because they don't have enough repeated, reinforced practice of skills to the point that they are truly mastered or *fluent*. Students fail because teachers aren't trained in how to create faultless communications in their presentation of curriculum. Students fail because the curriculum being used is poorly designed and the content inadequate. Students fail because they aren't encouraged or required to engage in lessons, and they aren't provided with immediate, specific feedback regarding their performance. Students fail because they never receive effective training in looking and listening. Students fail because they learn bad habits that interfere with their learning effective habits. Students fail because progress monitoring is inadequate. Students fail because grades aren't valid measures of learning. Ultimately, students fail because teachers aren't trained in behavioral science and the Technology of Teaching.

Moving forward requires a willingness to let go of the entrenched beliefs that promulgate ineffective educational practices. We must let go of the belief in inherent, mythical causes for learning or the failure to learn. We must let go of the belief that *naming* things also explains them. We must let go of the belief that the brain alone dictates everything we do and learn. We must let go of the belief that age determines when and if children acquire skills. We must let go of the belief that academic skills are inherited traits that children are born with, which simply develop over time. We must let go of the belief in inherent talent, or lack of talent, as an explanation for academic success or failure.

Letting go of these beliefs leads us to the next requirement for moving forward. We must be willing to acknowledge our role in how things go. Being *responsible* can be really scary. When the learning environment is granted its rightful place as the primary cause for learning, that ultimately means that everyone in contact with that environment is also, in some way, responsible. As parents, we have to be willing to be fully responsible for our children's behavior and willing to acknowledge when we have accidentally reinforced the kinds of behaviors that eventually drive us completely nuts. It's much easier to blame those behaviors on developmental stages or on our kid's internal flaws or personalities. It's much harder to admit that, for our kid's behavior to change, we also have to change our own behavior. Being fully responsible is hard work.

Similarly, teachers have to be fully responsible when learners succeed *and* when they fail. However, with training in behavioral science and the Technology of Teaching, teachers can intentionally design instruction that produces success with all learners, which includes identifying when things aren't working and designing strategies that promote effective change. In the current state of affairs, academic failures either result in personal assaults on the teacher or reference to inherent problems with the child. Neither of these options leads to effective actions.

Being trained in behavioral science and the Technology of Teaching allows teachers to be 100% responsible, which yields an enormous amount of *power*. This kind of training creates the possibility for teachers to achieve all of the things they set about to accomplish when they chose to become teachers. Teachers are some of the greatest humanitarians on earth. They devote their lives to educating our nation's youth for very little in return. Teachers don't enter their profession in search of fame and fortune. They enter their profession to make a difference. Unfortunately, admirable values and honorable intentions don't necessarily translate into effective actions. Teachers have a right to the kind of training that will allow them to accomplish the heroic acts that led them to the profession in the first place.

Ultimately, moving forward requires us all to agree that education belongs in the realm of *science*. We must draw a line in the sand indicating where our beliefs end and science takes over, as we have done with respect to medicine. Education belongs on the science side of that line. The educational establishment has always existed as an ideological institution based on beliefs regarding what children need to learn and how they should learn it. The educational establishment is on a continual quest for agreement—collecting evidence that confirms their beliefs and disregarding that which contradicts those beliefs. The result is a dogmatic, intractable institution that has nothing to do with effectively educating kids and everything to do with proving itself *right*. As a result, our nation's schools have never evolved because evolution comes from scientific inquiry and pragmatic values, not dogmatic ones.

So, are we ready to say to the establishments, and ultimately to ourselves, that time is up? Is more than 80 years of academic failure enough to lead us away from belief and toward the solutions offered by science? Are we willing to declare enough is enough? I certainly hope so. Imagine a future where all children receive an education that is scientifically sound and technically precise. We all know what the advances in modern science have made possible for our species and our civilization. Think of what might be possible if those same advances were allowed to occur in education. I have a pretty good idea of what might be possible. I think we might end up *intentionally* producing many more truly remarkable people capable of saving the world.

So if you are a parent reading this book, I hope that what you have read will empower you to advocate for more effective teaching strategies before blindly assuming that something is *wrong* with your child when they struggle academically. Even better, I hope that it will empower you to find learning centers or schools based in behavioral science and the Technology of Teaching and access these services for your child if you can. I have included a list of such organizations in the appendix for this chapter. I also hope that you now recognize that you are not alone. A majority of children struggle academically. Children who sail through school without difficulty are the exception, not the norm, though the establishments will lead you to believe the opposite.

If you are a teacher reading this book, I hope that what you have read will empower you to demand training in behavioral science and the Technology of Teaching. You deserve to be trained as a scientist, armed with the scientific tools that will ensure your ability to accomplish the difficult task you are charged with each day: effectively educating our nation's youth. I hope you now realize the inadequacies of your training and the ineffectiveness of the traditions that dominate our nation's schools. The struggles you experience with your students are not your fault — these struggles are the result of inadequate training and having to teach inside an ineffective system. We would never expect an engineer to effectively design a bridge without training in the physical sciences; yet the establishment expects teachers to effectively educate children without training in behavioral science, which is the *science of learning*. I hope that, like me, you get angry and that this book empowers you to do whatever it takes to access this training for yourself. I have provided resources for training of this sort in the appendix for this chapter.

If you are a citizen or policymaker reading this book, I hope that what you have read empowers you to advocate and vote for systemic changes to our educational system. Although I have recommended *bottom-up* reforms starting at the level of teaching practices, effective teaching can't happen if the system doesn't support it. We need *top-down* policy changes that will support the *bottom-up* changes I have recommended. The entire system needs to change. We need voters and policymakers willing to take risks and challenge the status quo. I hope this book has inspired you to take effective action and move mountains, but more importantly, I hope that you are inspired to take that first step, which is to simply acknowledge that the system can change, that education can improve, and that behavioral science is the answer.

Alex was one of the lucky ones. His mom discovered Fit Learning and, as a result, Alex became a successful student. The moment his mom enrolled him with us, the course of his life changed forever. Imagine if she had never discovered Fit Learning. Who would Alex be at this moment? I ask that question with respect to all of the learners who have been transformed by my organization over the years. On the one hand, I become overwhelmed with pride and profound joy when I think about those children and the amazing lives they now have the opportunity to lead. On the other hand, I think about the millions of children who don't get the opportunity to have their lives transformed through behavioral science and the Technology of Teaching. It is those children who keep me awake at night. It is those children who I am fighting for every single day.

My dear friend, Chuck Merbitz, who was a brilliant behavioral scientist and Precision Teacher, used to say, "We're all in this together." He meant that how education goes impacts all of us. The future of our planet and the survival of our species largely depends on the effective education of future generations. But our current educational crisis suggests a bleak and worrisome future. We can no longer afford to base education on ideology and belief. Just as the many problems we face as a nation and a species require solutions offered by science, so does our educational crisis. We must bring behavioral science into the classroom. With this science comes love, hope, power and limitless possibilities for every student. What happens next is up to us. Ultimately, the future depends on all of us because we really are all in this . . . together.

APPENDIX

CHAPTER 1: The Crisis

1. Long-Term Trends in Achievement: 4th Graders

   a. 4th Grade Reading Trends

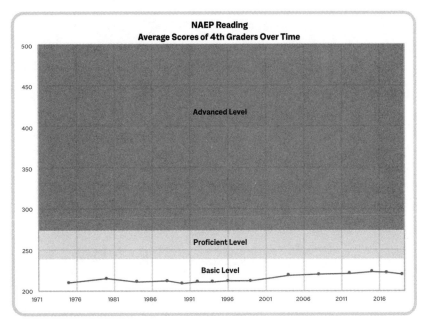

Figure A-1.

This figure reflects long-term trends in reading achievement for 4th graders from the first administration of the NAEP in 1971 to the most recent test conducted in 2019. Although modest gains in reading achievement have been made throughout this 48-year period, average scores for 4th graders have never exceeded the Basic level. Our educational system has failed to produce even minimal levels of proficiency in reading with a majority of 4th graders for almost five decades.

b. 4th Grade Math Trends

This figure reflects long-term trends in math achievement for 4th graders from the first administration of the NAEP in 1978 to the most recent test conducted in 2019. Although gains in math achievement have been made throughout this 48-year period, average scores for 4th graders have never exceeded the

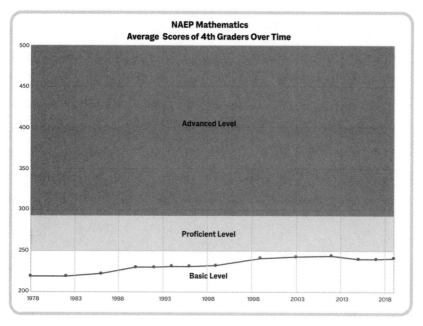

Figure A-2.

Basic level. Our educational system has failed to produce minimal levels of proficiency in math with a majority of 4th graders for almost five decades.

2. Long-Term Trends in Achievement: 8th Graders

    a. 8th Grade Reading Trends

    This figure reflects long-term trends in reading achievement for 8th graders from the first administration of the NAEP in 1971 to the most recent test conducted in 2019. The figure reflects that no lasting gains in reading achievement have been made throughout this 48-year period. Average scores for 8th graders have never exceeded the Basic level. Our educational system has failed to produce even minimal levels of proficiency in reading with a majority of 8th graders for almost five decades.

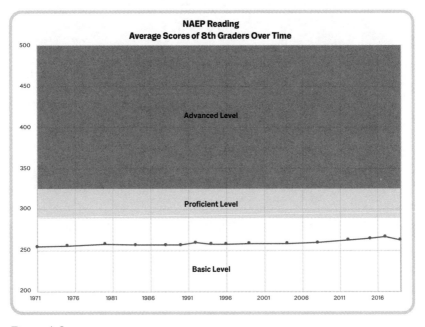

Figure A-3.

b. 8th Grade Math Trends

This figure reflects long-term trends in math achievement for 8th graders from the first administration of the NAEP in 1978 to the most recent test conducted in 2019. Although gains in math achievement have been made throughout this 48-year period, average scores for 8th graders have never exceeded the Basic level. Our educational system has failed to produce minimal levels of proficiency in math with a majority of 8th graders for almost five decades.

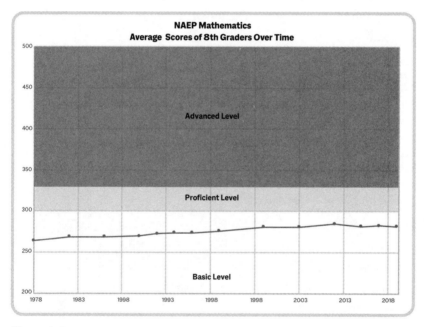

Figure A-4.

CHAPTER 7: The Evidence

3. Alex: 40-Hour Reading Skills Assessment

This figure reflects results from Alex's Reading Skills Assessment conducted at intake and after 40 hours of training at Fit Learning. The vertical axis reflects the average number correct per minute, so this figure reflects Alex's rate, or fluency, on the component skills for reading. The horizontal axis reflects the aggregate domains evaluated, with multiple subdomains included in each aggregate domain. Alex's performance on each subdomain is then aggregated to generate an average rate correct for that domain. The black horizontal lines that appear across the figure reflect the fluency aim for each domain. For

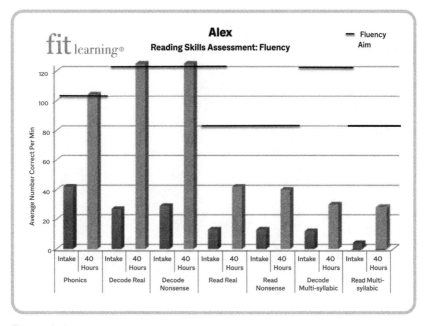

Figure A-5.

example, the fluency aim for Phonics is 100 correct per minute and so forth.

The figure reflects that at intake Alex was unable to fluently perform any component reading skills. Following 40 hours of training at Fit Learning, Alex showed significant improvements in his fluency across all component reading skills.

4. Alex: 40-Hour CBM Reading Assessments

This figure reflects Alex's 40-hour gains on CBM reading assessments (R-CBM) across three grade levels: Primer, 1st grade, and 2nd grade. When we initially assessed Alex, he was in 2nd grade; however, his grade-level CBM assessment indicated that he was reading below the first percentile. We also assessed a 1st grade level CBM to evaluate if his performance would improve at a lower grade level. Although he did read

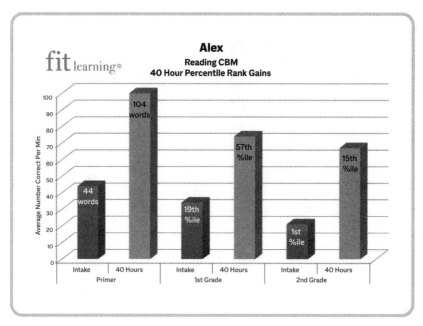

Figure A-6.

more words correctly, he scored in only the 19th percentile for 1st grade. Finally, we assessed him at the Primer level and identified that he read more words correctly, but even at the lowest assessment level, Alex was reading less than 45 words per minute. Primer level CBM does not provide information regarding national percentile rank.

Following 40 hours of training in component reading skills, Alex improved his reading rate from less than 45 words per minute to 100 words per minute on a Primer level reading CBM. He also increased from the 19th percentile to the 57th percentile for a 1st grade reading CBM and increased from the first percentile to the 15th percentile on a 2nd grade reading CBM. In other words, Alex showed dramatic gains across three reading levels, which equates to more than two years' worth of growth in 40 hours of training.

Each of Alex's figures reflect a portion of the progress data that I presented to Alex's school team during that notorious meeting I described in the introduction. These were the dramatic improvements in reading skills we had produced that the school team tried to refute. I hope you now have an even better understanding of his mom's frustration, and ultimately, why she eventually pulled him out of school altogether and enrolled him full-time at Fit Learning for that six-month period.

5. Program Analysis: Fit Learning Tristate

   a. Aggregate Gains on Reading Skills Assessment

   This figure reflects 40-hour gains made across core skills included in our Comprehensive Reading Skills Assessment obtained with 54 learners enrolled in our tristate locations (Locust Valley, New York; New York City; and Greenwich, Connecticut). As with Alex's reading skills assessment graph, the vertical axis reflects the average rate correct per minute. The

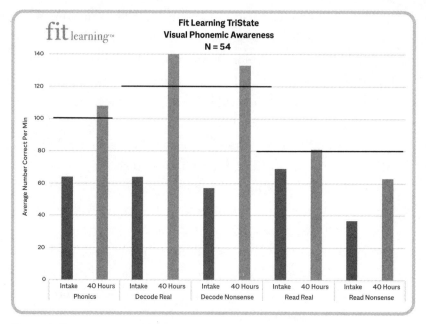

Figure A-7.

horizontal axis reflects the aggregate domains evaluated, and as previously described for Alex, there are multiple subdomains assessed within each aggregate domain and our learners' performances on each subdomain are then aggregated to generate an average rate correct per minute for that domain. Again, the horizontal lines that appear across the figure reflect the fluency aim for each domain.

As you can see from the figure, learners made significant gains in their fluency across core reading skills in 40 hours of training. On average, our learners achieved the fluency aim across all domains, with the exception of Reading Nonsense Words. These gains in fluency on component reading skills can then be compared with their percentile rank gain on CBM assessments, which appear below.

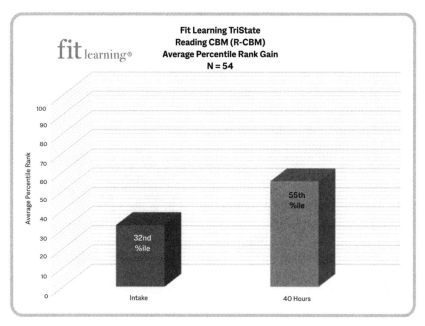

Figure A-8.

b. Aggregate Gains on CBM Reading Assessments

The Figure above reflects 40-hour gains in percentile rank on CBM reading assessments (R-CBM) conducted with the same 54 learners included in the Comprehensive Reading Skills Assessment figure. As we trained component reading skills to fluency, our learners made collateral gains on CBM assessments of reading. Learners enrolled in our tristate locations increased from the 32nd percentile to the 55th percentile on a standard measure of reading achievement. In other words, these learners gained 23 percentile ranks in 40 hours of reading training.

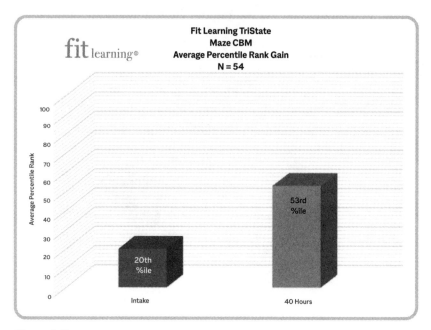

Figure A-9.

The figure above reflects 40-hour gains in percentile rank on a CBM Maze assessment obtained with the same 54 learners included in the Comprehensive Reading Skills Assessment figure. As we trained component reading skills to fluency, our learners made collateral gains on a CBM assessment of comprehension. Learners enrolled in our tristate locations increased from the 20th percentile to the 53rd percentile on a standard measure of reading achievement. In other words, these learners gained 33 percentile ranks on a measure of reading comprehension in 40 hours of reading training.

CHAPTER 8: The Future

Resources for Parents

Learning Centers and Schools Utilizing the Technology of Teaching [116]

Alabama

> JACKSONVILLE
>
> Jacksonville State University Learning Services: *jsu.edu/learningservices/*

Alaska

> GUSTAVUS
>
> Calkin Consulting Center, LLC: *www.abigailbcalkin.com*

Arizona

> LITCHFIELD PARK AND SCOTTSDALE
>
> Blossom Park, LLC (A Fit Learning Affiliate): *www.blossomparkza.com* or *www.fitlearning.com*
>
> PHOENIX
>
> Breakthrough Academy: *www.azbreakthroughacademy.org*

Arkansas

> LITTLE ROCK
>
> Innovative Behavior Analysis Support Systems, LLC: *www.innovativeaba.com*

California

> APTOS/SAN JOSE
>
> PALS (A Fit Learning Affiliate): *www.fitlearning.com*
>
> CLAREMONT
>
> Fit Learning: *www.fitlearning.com*

JACKSON
Haughton Learning Center:
www.haughtonlearningcenter.com

LOS ANGELES
Fit Learning: *www.fitlearning.com*

Colorado

ARVADA
Aim Learning & Educational Services:
www.aimlearning.net

COLORADO SPRINGS
Swift Behavioral, LLC: *www.swiftbehavioral.com*

DENVER
Fit Learning: *www.fitlearning.com*

Connecticut

GREENWICH
Fit Learning: *www.fitlearning.com*

WEST HARTFORD
Ben Bronz Academy: *www.benbronzacademy.org*

Florida

ORLANDO
Fit Learning: *www.fitlearning.com*

PENSACOLA
Fit Learning: *www.fitlearning.com*
Phoenix Learning Academy:
www.phoenixlearningacademy.org

Georgia

ATLANTA AND SANDY SPRINGS
Fit Learning: *www.fitlearning.com*

Hawaii

> HONOLULU
>
> Fit Learning: *www.fitlearning.com*

Illinois

> CHICAGO
>
> Fit Learning: *www.fitlearning.com*
>
> NAPERVILLE
>
> Fit Learning: *www.fitlearning.com*

Maine

> GRAY
>
> Burrow Consulting: *Drdot33@gmail.com*
>
> SABATTUS
>
> Regional School Union #4 (RSU #4):
> *www.rsu4.org*

Massachusetts

> HINGHAM
>
> The Fluency Factory: *www.fluencyfactory.com*

Missouri

> KANSAS CITY
>
> Fit Learning: *www.fitlearning.com*
>
> ST. LOUIS
>
> Fit Learning: *www.fitlearning.com*

Nebraska

> LINCOLN
>
> Fit Learning: *www.fitlearning.com*

Nevada

> RENO
>
> Fit Learning: *www.fitlearning.com*

New Hampshire
  STATHAM
  Precision Learning, LLC: https://*precisionlearningllc.com*

New Jersey
  BASKING RIDGE
  Fit Learning: *www.fitlearning.com*

New York
  LOCUST VALLEY
  Fit Learning: *www.fitlearning.com*

  UPPER EAST SIDE, MANHATTAN
  Fit Learning: *www.fitlearning.com*

North Carolina
  LELAND, SOUTHPORT, WHITEVILLE, & WILMINGTON
  Charter Day School/ Roger Bacon Academy:
    www.rogerbaconacademy.net

North Dakota
  FARGO
  Fit Learning: *www.fitlearning.com*

Ohio
  CIRCLEVILLE
  Inspiration Tutoring: *Inspirationtutoring2013@gmail.com*

  CLEVELAND
  Fit Learning: *www.fitlearning.com*

Oregon
  LAKE OSWEGO
  Fit Learning: *www.fitlearning.com*

  ROSEBURG
  Learning Matters: *www.learningmattersnow.com*

Pennsylvania

    COOPERSBURG

    Smart Spot Educational Services, LLC:
    www.smartspotlearning.com

    PITTSBURGH

    AIMS: Agile Instruction and Management Solutions:
    www.aimsintruction.com

Texas

    AUSTIN

    Fit Learning: *www.fitlearning.com*
    The Magnolia School:
    www.themagnoliaschoolatx.com

    DENTON
    The Koan School: *www.koanschool.org*

Utah

    SALT LAKE CITY
    Fit Learning: *www.fitlearning.com*

Virginia

    SALEM & ROANOKE
    Fit Learning: *www.fitlearning.com*

Washington, D.C.

    Fit Learning: *www.fitlearning.com*

Washington

    SEATTLE

    Morningside Academy: *www.morningsideacademy.org*

    WOODINVILLE

    Dolan Academy and Learning Center:
    www.dolanlearning.com

Wisconsin
>   WAUWATOSA
>   Tosa Learning Center: *maryschmidt@me.com*

Australia
>   PERTH (CLAREMONT & COTTESOLE)
>   Fit Learning: *www.fitlearning.com.au* or *www.fitlearning.com*

Botswana
>   Ambrose Academy: *www.ambroseacademy.co.bw*

Canada
>   ONTARIO
>   QLC Educational Services: *Michael@maloneymethod.com*
>   Step by Step Learning Group: *www.sbslg.com*
>
>   TORONTO
>   Fit Learning: *www.fitlearning.com*
>
>   VANCOUVER, BC
>   Fit Learning: *www.fitlearning.ca* or *www.fitlearning.com*

England
>   KENT
>   Precision Teaching Kent: *www.precisionteachingkent.com*

Iceland
>   REYKJAVIK
>   Behavior Analysis & Teaching Consultation:
>   *adda@ismennt.is*

Italy
>   CASTEL SAN GIOVANNI, PIACENZA, RUBIERA, CORREGGIO
>   Centro TICE Learning Centers: *www.centrotice.it*

Wales
>   ARDDOL, DOLYDD, & GWYNEDD
>   Bethan Mair Williams: *Bethan.mair@tiscali.co.uk*

Resources for Educators

Professional Societies/Organizations/Resources

Society for Standard Celeration: *www.celeration.org*

The Fluency Project: *www.fluency.org*

Cambridge Center for Behavioral Studies: *www.behavior.org*

National Institute for Direct Instruction: *www.nifdi.org*

Association for Behavior Analysis International:
www.abainternational.org

Conferences

International Precision Teaching Conference

National Institute for Direct Instruction Conference

Annual Conference of the Association for Behavior Analysis
International

Workshops/Training Opportunities

Fit Learning Affiliate Certification: *www.fitlearning.com*

Praxis, Scientist-Educator Workshop Series:
www.praxiscet.com/workshops/

Morningside Academy, Summer Teachers' Institute:
www.morningsideacademy.org

Morningside Model School-Wide Trainings:
www.morningsideacademy.org

Central Reach Precision X (Chartlytics):
www.centralreach.com/precisionx/

National Institute for Direct Instruction: *www.nifdi.org*; follow
links for Services

AimsWeb Plus: *www.pearsonassessments.com*; follow links for
CBM and Training

REFERENCES

1. National Center for Education Statistics, National Assessment of Educational Progress. *https://nces.ed.gov/nationsreportcard/*.

2. Skinner, B. F., The technology of teaching. The Century psychology series. 1968, New York: Appleton-Century-Crofts. ix, 271 pp.

3. Barrett, B. H., The technology of teaching revisited: A reader's companion to B. F. Skinner's book. 2002, Concord, MA: Cambridge Center for Behavioral Studies. vi, 133 pp.

4. Bestor, A. E., Educational wastelands: The retreat from learning in our public schools. 1953, Urbana: University of Illinois Press. 226 pp.

5. Cremin, L. A., The transformation of the school; Progressivism in American education, 1876–1957. 1st ed. 1961, New York: Knopf. 387 pp.

6. Koerner, J. D., The miseducation of American teachers. 1963, Boston: Houghton Mifflin. 360 pp.

7. Barret, B. H., Beck, R., Binder, C. et al., The right to effective education. The Behavior Analyst, 1991. 14: pp. 79–82.

8. Watkins, C. L., Project Follow Through: A case study of contingencies influencing instructional practices of the educational establishment. Behavior monographs. 1997, Cambridge, MA: Cambridge Center for Behavioral Studies. viii, 103 pp.

9. Binder, C., Watkins, C. L., Precision Teaching and Direct Instruction: Measurably superior instructional technology in schools. Performance Improvement Quarterly 1990. 3(4): pp.74 - 96.

10. Meyer, S., Newsome, D., Fuller, T., Newsome, K., Agility: What is it, how to measure it, and how to use it. Behavior Analysis in Practice, in press.

11. Johnson, K. R., E. M. Street, and Morningside Academy (Seattle, WA), The Morningside model of generative instruction: What it means to leave no child behind. 2004, Concord, MA: Cambridge Center for Behavioral Studies. 236 pp.

12. Berens, K., Boyce, T. E., Berens, N. M., Doney, J. K., Kenzer, A .L., A technology for evaluating relations between response frequency and academic performance outcomes. Journal of Precision Teaching and Celeration, 2003. 19(1): pp. 20–34.

13. Engelmann, S., Direct instruction. The Instructional design library v. 22. 1980, Englewood Cliffs, NJ: Educational Technology Publications. xii, 111 pp.

14. Kozol, J., The shame of a nation: The restoration of apartheid schooling in America. 2005, New York: Random House.

15. Kozol, J., Savage inequalities: Children in America's schools. 1991, New York: Crown Publishing. ix, 262 pp.

16. Dickens, P., Social Darwinism: Linking evolutionary thought to social theory. Concepts in the social sciences. 2000, Buckingham, England; Philadelphia: Open University Press. 135 pp.

17. Herrnstein, R. J. and C. A. Murray, The bell curve: Intelligence and class structure in American life. 1994, New York: Free Press. xxvi, 845 pp.

18. Hofstadter, R. and American Historical Association, Social Darwinism in American thought, 1860-1915. 1944, Philadelphia: University of Pennsylvania Press; H. Milford, Oxford University Press. viii pp., 1 l.

19. Hart, B. and T. R. Risley, Meaningful differences in the everyday experience of young American children. 1995, Baltimore: P.H. Brookes. xxiii, 268 pp.

20. Schwarz, A., ADHD nation: Children, doctors, big pharma, and the making of an American epidemic. 2016, New York: Scribner. viii, 338 pages.

21. Coles, G., The learning mystique: A critical look at "learning disabilities." 1987, New York: Pantheon Books. xvii, 330 pp.

22. National Center for Learning Disabilities, *https://www.ncld.org/archives/blog/the-state-of-ld-understanding-the-1-in-5.*

23. Individuals with Disabilities Education Act, *https://sites.ed.gov/idea/.*

24. Jacoby, S., The age of American unreason in a culture of lies. New updated edition. 2018, New York: Vintage Books, xxviii, 364 pages.

25. Ericsson, K. A., Pool, R., Peak: Secrets from the new science of expertise. 2016, Boston, MA: Houghton Mifflin Harcourt.

26. Ravitch, D., The death and life of the great American school system: How testing and choice are undermining education. 2010: Basic Books.

27. Ravitch, D., The great school wars: A history of the New York City public schools. Johns Hopkins University Paperbacks ed. 2000, Baltimore, Md.: Johns Hopkins University Press. xxxviii, 449 pp.

28. Ravitch, D., Reign of error: The hoax of the privatization movement and the danger to America's public schools. 2013, New York: Knopf. xii, 396 pages.

29. United States National Commission on Excellence in Education, A nation at risk : The imperative for educational reform: A report to the nation and the Secretary of Education, United States Department of Education. 1983, Washington, D.C.: The Commission: Supt. of Docs., U.S. G.P.O. distributor. V., 65 pp.

30. Lund, L., Conference Board., and United States National Commission on Excellence in Education, Ten years after A Nation at Risk. Report / The Conference Board. 1993, New York: Conference Board. 29 pp.

31. Vinovskis, M., From a nation at risk to No Child Left Behind: National education goals and the creation of federal education policy. 2009, New York: Teachers College Press. xiv, 297 pp.

32. National Center for Education Statistics, Program for International Student Assessment, https://nces.ed.gov/surveys/pisa/.

33. Ripley, A., The smartest kids in the world: And how they got that way. 2013, New York: Simon & Schuster. 306 pp.

34. Chu, L., Little soldiers: An American boy, A Chinese school, and the global race to achieve. 2017, New York: HarperCollins.

35. Sykes, C. J., Dumbing down our kids: Why America's children feel good about themselves but can't read, write, or add. 1995, New York: St. Martin's Press. x, 341 pp.

36. Hofstadter, R., Anti-intellectualism in American life. 1st ed., 1963, New York: Knopf. 434, xiii p.

37. Hofstadter, R., The Progressive movement, 1900–1915. 1st Touchstone ed. 1986, New York: Simon & Schuster. 185 pp.

38. Mann, H., Education and prosperity. Old South leaflets, General series. 1903, Boston: Directors of the Old South Work. 20 pp.

39. Mann, H., Lectures on education. 1850, Boston: L.N. Ide. x, 11 -338 pp.

40. Dewey, J., The school and society. 3d ed. 1900, Chicago: The University of Chicago Press; McClure, Phillips & Company. 129 pp., 1 l.

41. Dewey, J., Democracy and education: An introduction to the philosophy of education. Textbook series in education. 1916, New York: Macmillan. xii, p., 1 l., 434 pp.

42. Dewey, J., The child and the curriculum. 1902, Chicago: University of Chicago Press. 40 pp.

43. Dewey, J., Moral principles in education. Riverside educational monographs. 1909, Boston, New York: Houghton Mifflin Company. ix, 1 p., 1 l., 60, 2 p.

44. Cardinal principles of secondary education: A report of the Commission on the Reorganization of Secondary Education, appointed by the National Education Association. In Bulletin (United States, Bureau of Education) 1918, no. 35.

45. James, W., The principles of psychology. American science-advanced course. 1890, New York: Henry Holt & Company.

46. James, W., Pragmatism, a new name for some old ways of thinking. 1907, New York: Longmans, Green, and Company. xii, 1, 308, 2 p.

47. Bijou, S. W., Child development: The basic stage of early childhood. The Century psychology series. 1976, Englewood Cliffs, NJ: Prentice-Hall. xiii, 210 pp.

48. Hall, G. S., Adolescence. 1904, New York: Appleton.

49. Hall, G. S., The contents of children's minds on entering school. 1893, New York and Chicago: E. L.. Kellogg & Co. 56 pp.

50. Hall, G. S., Educational problems. 1911, New York, London: Appleton.

51. Hall, G. S., How to teach reading, and what to read in school. 1886, Boston: D. C. Heath & Co. 1 p. l., 40 pp.

52. Hall, G. S. and T. L. Smith, Aspects of child life and education. 1907, Boston: Ginn. ix, 326 pp.

53. Piaget, J., Science of education and the psychology of the child. 1970, New York: Orion Press. 186 pp.

54. Piaget, J., The psychology of intelligence. International library of psychology, philosophy and scientific method. 1950, London: Routledge & Kegan Paul. viii, 182 pp.

55. Piaget, J., The origin of intelligence in the child. 1953, London: Routledge & Kegan Paul. 425 pp.

56. Piaget, J., The child's construction of reality. 1954, London: Routledge & Kegan Paul. xiii, 386 pp.

57. Piaget, J., H. E. Gruber, and J. J. Vonèche, The essential Piaget. 100th Anniversary ed. 1995, Northvale, NJ: J. Aronson. xliv, 912 pp.

58. Piaget, J. and B. Inhelder, The psychology of the child. 1969, New York: Basic Books. xiv, 173 pp.

59. Bijou, S. W. and D. M. Baer, Behavior analysis of child development. The Century psychology series. 1978, Englewood Cliffs, NJ: Prentice-Hall. xii, 132 pp.

60. Bijou, S. W. and D. M. Baer, Child development. The Century psychology series. 1961, New York: Appleton-Century-Crofts.

61. Bijou, S. W., D. M. Baer, and A. Anastasi, Child development; Readings in experimental analysis. The Century psychology series. 1967, New York: Appleton-Century-Crofts. ix, 408 pp.

62. Bijou, S. W. and E. Ribes Iñesta, Behavior modification; Issues and extensions. 1972, New York: Academic Press. xii, 157 pp.

63. Bijou, S. W. and R. Ruíz, Behavior modification: Contributions to education. 1981, Hillsdale, NJ: L. Erlbaum Associates. viii, 312 pp.

64. Sagan, C., The demon-haunted world: Science as a candle in the dark. 1st ed. 1995, New York: Random House. xviii, 457 pp.

65. Thorndike, E. L., Empirical studies in the theory of measurement. Archives of psychology. 1907, New York: The Science Press. 2 p. l., 45 pp.

66. Thorndike, E. L., Education, a first book. 1912, New York: Macmillan. ix, 292 pp.

67. Thorndike, E. L., Educational psychology. American education — Its men, ideas, and institutions. 1969, New York: Arno Press.

68. Thorndike, E. L. and W. C. Bagley, Education as cause and as symptom. The Kappa Delta Pi lecture series No 11. 1939, New York: Macmillan. xiii, 1 , 92 pp.

69. Thorndike, E. L., and A. I. Gates, Elementary principles of education. 1929, New York: Macmillan. x, 335 pp.

70. Terman, L. M., The intelligence of school children: How children differ in ability, the use of mental tests in school grading and the proper education of exceptional children. Riverside textbooks in education. 1919, Boston: Houghton, Mifflin & Company. xxii, 317 pp.

71. Terman, L. M., The measurement of intelligence. Classics in child development. 1975, New York: Arno Press. xviii, 362 pp.

72. Terman, L. M., and National Education Association of the United States. Commission on Revision of Elementary Education, Intelligence tests and school reorganization. 1922, Yonkers-on-Hudson, NY: World Book Company. viii, 111 pp.

73. Doidge, N., The brain that changes itself: Stories of personal triumph from the frontiers of brain science. 2007, New York: Viking. xvi, 427 pp.

74. Doidge, N., The brain's way of healing: Remarkable discoveries and recoveries from the frontiers of neuroplasticity. Updated and expanded edition. 2016, New York: Penguin Books. xx, 427 pp.

75. Meyler, A., Keller, T. A., Cherkassky, V. L., Gabrieli, J. D. E., & Just, M. A., Modifying the brain activation of poor readers during sentence comprehension with extended remedial instruction: A longitudinal study of neuroplasticity. Neuropsychologia 2008. 46: pp. 2580–2592.

76. Jasanoff, A., The biological mind: How brain, body, and environment collaborate to make us who we are. 2018, New York: Basic Books. p. 1 online resource.

77. Klein, J. A. J., T. A., Principles in experience-dependent neural plasticity: Implications for rehabilitation after brain damage. Journal of Speech, Language, and Hearing Research 2008. 51: pp. S225–S238.

78. Aylward, E. H., Richards, T. L., Berninger, V. W., Nagy, W. E., Field, K. M., Grimme, A. C., Richards, B. S., Thomson, J. B., & Cramer, S. C., Instructional treatment associated with changes in brain activation in children with dyslexia. Neurology 2003. 61: pp. 212–219.

79. Eden, G. F., Jones, K. M., Cappell, K., Gareau, L., Wood, F. B., Zeffiro, T. A., Dietz, N. A., Agnew, J. A., & Flowers, D. L, Neural changes following remediation in adult developmental dyslexia. Neuron 2004. 44: pp. 411–422.

80. Temple, E., Deutsch, G. K., Poldrack, R. A., Miller, S. L., Tallal, P., Merzenich, M. M., Gabrieli, J. D, Neural deficits in children with dyslexia ameliorated by behavioral remediation: Evidence from functional MRI. Proceedings from the National Academy of Sciences of the United States of America 2003. 5: pp. 2860–2865.

81. Keller, T. A., .Just, M. A., Altering cortical activity: Remediation-induced changes in the white matter of poor readers. Neuron, 2009. 64: pp. 624–631

82. Hofstadter, R. and B. K. Hofstadter, Great issues in American history: From Reconstruction to the present day, 1864–1981. Rev. ed. 1982, New York: Vintage Books. xv, 602 pp.

83. Skinner, B. F., The behavior of organisms. 1938, New York: Appleton-Century-Crofts. xv, 457 pp.

84. Skinner, B. F., About behaviorism. 1st ed. 1974, New York: Knopf.

85. Skinner, B. F., Science and human behavior. 1953, New York: Macmillan. 461 pp.

86. Thorndike, E. L., Animal intelligence: An experimental study of the associative processes in animals. 1898, New York , London: Macmillan. 109 pp.

87. Thorndike, E. L., Animal intelligence; Experimental studies. 1911, New York: Macmillan.

88. Johnston, J. M. and H. S. Pennypacker, Strategies and tactics of human behavioral research. 1980, Hillsdale, NJ: L. Erlbaum Associates. xvi, 472 pp.

89. Skinner, B. F., Verbal behavior. The Century psychology series. 1957, New York: Appleton-Century-Crofts. 478 pp.

90. Hayes, S. C., D. Barnes-Holmes, and B. Roche, Relational frame theory: A post-Skinnerian account of human language and cognition. 2001, New York: Kluwer Academic/Plenum Publishers. xvii, 285 pp.

91. Ferster, C. B. S., B. F. Skinner , Schedules of reinforcement 1957, Acton, MA: Copley Publishing Group.

92. Skinner, B. F., Beyond freedom and dignity. 1st ed. 1971, New York: Knopf. 225 pp.

93. Skinner, B. F., The phylogeny and ontogeny of behavior. Science, 1966. 153(3741): pp. 1205–1213.

94. Keller, F. S., Learning: reinforcement theory. 2d ed. A Random House study in psychology, PP13. 1969, New York: Random House. 82 pp.

95. Keller, F. S., The definition of psychology; An introduction to psychological systems. The Century psychology series. 1937, New York, London: D. Appleton-Century Company. vi p., 2 l., 111 pp.

96. Keller, F. S. and E. Ribes Iñesta, Behavior modification: Applications to education. 1974, New York: Academic Press. xvi, 211 p.

97. Keller, F. S., and W. N. Schoenfeld, Principles of psychology; A systematic text in the science of behavior. The Century psychology series. 1950, New York: Appleton-Century-Crofts. xv, 431 pp.

98. Dymond, S., and B. Roche, Advances in relational frame theory: Research & application. 2013, Oakland, CA: Context Press. xii, 281 pages.

99. Berens, N. M., Hayes, S. C., Arbitrarily applicable comparative relations: Experimental evidence for relational operants. Journal of Applied Behavior Analysis, 2007. 40: pp. 45–71.

100. Newsome, K., Berens, K., Ghezzi, P., Aninao, T., Newsome, W. D., Training relational language to improve comprehension. European Journal of Behavior Analysis, 2015. 15(2).

101. Pryor, K., Don't shoot the dog: The art of teaching and training. First trade paperback edition, 2019, New York: Simon & Schuster. xix, 213 pages.

102. Pennypacker, H. S., Gutierrez, A., Lindsley, O. R., Handbook of the Standard Celeration Chart. 2003, Cambridge, MA: Cambridge Center for Behavioral Studies.

103. CentralReach PrecisionX [Computer software]. 2019. Retrieved from *https://centralreach.com.*

104. Adams, G. L., and S. Engelmann, Research on direct instruction: 25 years beyond DISTAR. 1996, Seattle, WA: Educational Achievement System. x, 146 pp.

105. Binder, C., Behavioral fluency: Evolution of a new paradigm. The Behavior Analyst, 1996. 19(2): pp. 163–197.

106. Ervin, R. A.; DuPaul, G. J; Kern, L.; Friman, P.C., Classroom-based functional and adjunctive assessments: Proactive approaches to intervention selection for adolescents with Attention Deficit Hyperactivity Disorder. Journal of Applied Behavior Analysis, 1998. 31(1): pp. 65–78.

107. Flood, W. A., Wilder, D. A., Flood, A. L., Masuda, A., Peer-mediated reinforcement plus prompting as treatment for off-task behavior in children with Attention Deficit Hyperactivity Disorder. Journal of Applied Behavior Analysis, 2002. 35(2): pp. 199–204.

108. Mayville, E. A., and J. A. Mulick, Behavioral foundations of effective autism treatment. The Cambridge Center-Sloan century series in behavior analysis. 2011, Cornwall-on-Hudson, NY: Sloan Publishing. x, 351 pp.

109. Roane, H. S., Fisher, W. W., Carr, J. E., Applied behavior analysis as treatment for autism spectrum disorder. The Journal of Pediatrics 2016. 175: pp. 27–32.

110. Rosenwasser, B., Axelrod, S., More contributions of applied behavior analysis to the education of people with autism. Behavior Modification 2002. 26(1): pp. 3–8.

111. Rosenwasser, B., Axelrod, S., The contributions of applied behavior analysis to the education of people with autism. Behavior Modification, 2001. 25(5): pp. 671–677.

112. Lindsley, O. R., From Skinner to Precision Teaching: The child knows best. The Council for Exceptional Children 1971: pp. 2–11.

113. Binder, C., Haughton, E. C., & Van Eyk, D. , Increasing endurance by building fluency: Precision Teaching attention span. Teaching Exceptional Children 1990. 22(3): pp. 24–27.

114. Johnson, K. R., Layng, T. J, Breaking the structuralist barrier: Literacy and numeracy with fluency. American Psychologist, 1992. 47(11): pp. 1475–1490.

115. Kubina, R. Jr., R. S. Morrison, Fluency In education. Behavior and Social Issues, 2000. 10: pp. 83–99.

116. N. G. Haring, M. S. White, M. D. Neely, eds., Precision Teaching: A practical science of education. 2019, Cornwall-on-Hudson, NY: Sloan Publishing.

117. Binder, C., Precision Teaching and curriculum-based measurement. Journal of Precision Teaching, 1990. 7(2): pp. 33–35.

118. Binder, C, Watkins, C. L., Precision Teaching: Measuring and attaining exemplary academic achievement. Youth Policy Journal, 1988. 10(7): pp. 12–15.

119. Johnson, K. R., Response to intervention and Precision Teaching: Creating synergy in the classroom. 2013, New York: Guilford Press. xvii, 205 pp.

120. Kunzelmann, H. P., M. A. Cohen, and University of Washington Child Development and Mental Retardation Center, Experimental Education Unit. Precision Teaching; An initial training sequence. 1970, Seattle, WA: Special Child Publications. 310 pp.

121. Lindsley, O. R., Precision Teaching: By teachers for children. Teaching Exceptional Children, 1990. 22(3): pp. 10–15.

122. Lindsley, O. R., Precision Teaching's unique legacy from B. F. Skinner. Journal of Behavioral Education 1991. 1(2): pp. 253–266.

123. Lindsley, O. R., Precision Teaching: Discoveries and effects. Journal of Applied Behavior Analysis, 1992. 25(1): pp. 51–57.

124. Lindsley, O. R., Celeration and agility for the 2000s. Journal of Precision Teaching, 2000. 17(2): pp. 107–111.

125. Haughton, E., Aims — Growing and Sharing. 1972, Invisible College Conference on Application of Behavioral Principles in Exceptional Child Education, Arlington, VA. pp. 20–39.

126. Milyko, K., Berens, K., Ghezzi, P., An Investigation of rapid automatic naming as a generalized operant. Journal of Precision Teaching and Celeration, 2012. 28(3): pp. 3–16.

127. Kohn, A., Punished by rewards: The trouble with gold stars, incentive plans, A's, praise, and other bribes. Twenty-fifth anniversary edition. 2018, Boston: Houghton Mifflin Company. xii, 466 pages.

128. Adams, L. S., Five methods of serial rote learning: A comparative study. 1938, New York: Columbia University, p. 67, 1 p. incl. tables.

129. A. Whimbey, J. Lochhead., & R. Narode, Problem solving and comprehension. 7th ed. 2013, New York and London: Routledge.

130. Carnine, D., Direct Instruction reading. 4th ed. 2004, Upper Saddle River, NJ: Pearson Prentice Hall. xiv, 397 pp.

131. Silbert, J., D. Carnine, and M. Stein, Direct Instruction mathematics. 2nd ed. 1990, Columbus, OH: C.E. Merrill Publishing Company. xvii, 508 pp.

132. Wood, T. W., Engelmann's direct instruction: Selected writings from the past half century. 2014, Eugene, OR: NIFDI Press. 467 pp.

133. Howard, E. D., Developing intelligence by the Socratic method. The Socratic institute Guide book, Preliminary ed. 1923, Chicago: The Socratic institute. Publication division. 2 p. l., vi, 169 pp.

134. Deno, S., Curriculum-based measurement: The emerging alternative. Exceptional Children 1985. 52: pp. 219–232.

135. Deno, S., Whither thou goest: Perspectives on progress monitoring. In J. W. Lloyd, E. J. Kameenui, D. Chard, eds., Issues in Educating Students with Disabilities. 1997, Mahwah, NJ: L Erlbaum Associates, pp. 77–99.

136. Deno, S., Developments in curriculum-based measurement. The Journal of Special Education 2003. 37(7): pp. 184–192.

137. *https://app.aimswebplus.com.*

138. Bradfield, R. H., Behavior modification of learning disabilities. 1971, San Rafael, CA: Academic Therapy Publications. 172 pp.

139. Moran, D. J., and R. W. Malott, Evidence-based educational methods. Educational psychology series. 2004, San Diego, CA.: Elsevier Academic Press. xxiv, 382 pp.

140. Lovitt, T. C., N. G. Haring, and University of Washington. Child Development and Mental Retardation Center, Experimental Education Unit., Classroom application of precision teaching. 1979, Seattle, WA: Special Child Publications. 155 pp.

141. Meacham, M. L., and A. E. Wiesen, Changing classroom behavior; A manual for precision teaching. 1969, Scranton,PA: International Textbook Co. vii, 212 pp.

142. Espin, C., A measure of success: The influence of curriculum-based measurement on education. 2012, Minneapolis: University of Minnesota Press. xiii, 392 pp.

143. Hosp, M. K., J. L. Hosp, and K. W. Howell, The abcs of CBM: A practical guide to curriculum-based measurement. 2007, New York: Guilford Press. x, 172 pp.

144. Lindsley, O. R., Direct measurement and prosthesis of retarded behavior. Journal of Education 1964. 147: pp. 62–28.

145. Lindsley, O. R., Operant conditioning methods applied to research in chronic schizophrenia. Psychiatric Research Reports 1956. 5: pp. 118–139.

146. Azrin, N. H., Lindsley, O. R., The reinforcement of cooperation between children. Journal of Abnormality and Social Psychology 1956. 52(1): pp. 100–103.

147. Koenig, C., The behavior bank: A system for sharing precise information. Teaching Exceptional Children, 1971 3(3): pp. 157.

ACKNOWLEDGMENTS

This book is dedicated to my beloved undergraduate mentor, Maria Ruiz, who left us much too soon. My life changed forever the moment she walked into my Introduction to Psychology class during my first semester of freshman year. She was the smallest woman I had ever seen, but then she started speaking and became larger than life. Maria taught me to think critically, to fight for those who couldn't fight for themselves, and to work tirelessly in bringing our science forward for the benefit of all humanity. Not a day goes by that I don't think of her and silently thank her for the profound contribution she made to my life.

I owe a profound debt to the entire faculty in the Behavior Analysis Program at the University of Nevada — Reno who supported our Precision Teaching project from the very beginning. My deepest thanks go to Ted Boyce, who provided me with invaluable mentorship during those early years. I also owe thanks to Linda Hayes, Steve Hayes, Sid Bijou, Jim Carr, Larry Williams, Pat Friman, Ramona Houmanfar, Michelle Wallace, and in particular, my hero and dear friend, Pat Ghezzi. I also owe thanks to all of the graduate students, in particular Christine Kim Walton and Brian Gaunt, who helped to get our program going in the first place.

Thank you to the many members of the Precision Teaching community who have provided me with support and mentorship throughout my career. I owe my deepest thanks to Carl Binder, Kent Johnson, Elizabeth Haughton, Abigail Calkin, Dennis Eddinger, Hank Pennypacker, Rick Kubina, Pat McGreevy, John Eshleman, Malcolm Neely, Mike Fabrizio, and our beloved Chuck Merbitz. Fit Learning exists because of all of you. Additional thanks to Mal Neely for assisting with the list of organizations and schools that appears in the appendix — such an invaluable resource for parents and educators!

It is difficult for me to properly express my gratitude for Ogden Lindsley. Og also changed my life forever, beginning with a conversation in an airport when we happened to be on the same flight, and the flight happened to be very delayed. From that moment on, he became my mentor and dear friend. Og made me a scientist and led me to discover the love that comes from our science. He armed me with the tools required to maintain precision while making broad-scale impacts. His legacy made it possible for Fit Learning to transform hundreds of learners each year. Not a day goes by that I don't say to myself, "Thanks, Og."

I am lucky to have the most amazing partners in the universe. Thank you to Nick Berens, Kendra Newsome, and Donny Newsome — you all inspire me to be better, to live inside our values every day, and to work tirelessly in service of this vision we realized many years ago. Thank you to our gentle wrangler, Pete Skeffington. Your leadership and wisdom has enabled us to realize our vision and take Fit Learning to the next level. Thank you to my entire team in the tristate region and, in particular, Phil Cairoli, Christina Cairoli, Kaitlin LaBarbera, Elle

Kirsten, and Allison Segal. Your passion, dedication, and work ethic take my breath away on a daily basis. To all of the dazzling scientist-educators working in Fit Learning locations around the globe — thank you for jumping off the cliff with us, upholding our values, trusting the science, and believing in our vision. I am so thankful to be on this journey with all of you. In particular, thank you to Mandy Mason, our fearless leader in Australia, whose friendship I cherish and from whom I have learned so much.

Thank you to my publicists, Robyn Ungar and Alana Cohen, who so skillfully ensure that our important message gets out to the public. Thank you to my entire team at The Collective Book Studio who worked tirelessly to get my book out to the world in record time. Thank you to Angela Engel for starting a publishing house that truly supports writers and creates such a wonderfully collaborative process. I'm so glad I came across your blog that day! Thank you to Elisabeth Saake for reading my book cover to cover in one sitting and realizing the importance of its message. Thank you to my lead editor, Lee Bruno, whose wisdom and gentle guidance led me to transform my original academic manuscript into a book that appeals to all readers. Finally, thank you to Dean Burrell for your attention to detail and overall refinement of the book.

Finally, I am deeply thankful for my family. Thanks to my mom for teaching me how to work hard and for always believing in me, particularly when others didn't. Thanks to my mother-in-law, Liz, for the years of love, support, friendship, and, most important, golf! Thank you to my children, Emma and Jack, who are the light of my life. I know I wasn't always fun to be around and often I wasn't around at all — thanks for loving me anyway. Nick — I have thanked you as my partner in work, and now I must thank you as my partner in life. The first time I won the metaphorical lottery is when I met you. You are my soul mate, my best friend, my sounding board, my sanity, my comic relief and . . . my golf buddy. This book wouldn't have happened without you.

INDEX